Housing Policy & the Urban Middle Class

Housing Policy & the Urban Middle Class

Kristina Ford

Preface by
ALLAN R. TALBOT
and
Introduction by
GEORGE STERNLIEB

Published jointly by
Center for Urban Policy Research
&
Citizens Housing and Planning
Council of New York

The Center for Urban Policy Research
P.O. Box 38
New Brunswick, New Jersey 08903

Kristina Ford has a Ph.d. in Urban and Regional Planning from The University of Michigan. This book was written while she was a Research Assistant Professor at the Center for Urban Policy Research, Rutgers University.

Cover design by Francis G. Mullen.
Graphics by Frank Gradilone

Published in the United States of America by the Center for Urban Policy Research, New Brunswick, New Jersey 08903

ISBN: 0-88285-056-3

Richard

Contents

List of Exhibits

CHAPTER 1

CHAPTER 2

CHAPTER 3

CHAPTER 4

CHAPTER 5

Preface

In 1975, at the height of public awareness of New York City's money problems, the city government made economic development a major priority for municipal programs. The need was obvious. New York had to pay more attention to private sector employment as a way of maintaining or, hopefully, augmenting jobs and tax revenues.

One major area of local governmental activity -- city housing policy -- escaped much notice. That is probably because housing has traditionally been viewed as a problem or a need, with its major economic contribution popularly regarded as a short-term stimulus to the construction industry.

Yet the city's housing and neighborhood policies can play a larger and longer-term role in economic development. Employers count the availability and proximity of good housing and neighborhoods as a factor in their location decisions. At the same time, the city economy is helped if housing policies increase the number of city residents, specifically those who spend far more in private goods and services in New York than they demand in services or payments supported by the city treasury.

So, in very practical terms, the following housing policy question arises: How, and at what cost, can the city induce greater numbers of its workforce, current and projected, to live here?

Beginning in September 1977, the Citizens Housing and Planning Council and the Center for Urban Policy Research addressed this question on a number of related fronts. We began by examining what kind of housing demand is liable to be generated by the projected work force through 1985. We also evaluated current city housing strategies to determine how they work both in terms of their costs to the city and their benefits in attracting or retaining the city work force as residents. Finally, through a survey of commuters, we looked at the possibilities of a return to the city by suburbanites to determine what kinds of housing might encourage more of them to live in New York.

The aim of these efforts, which were supported by the Rockefeller Brothers Fund, the New York State Division of Housing and Community Renewal, and the Ford Foundation, is to suggest what kinds of policies and programs will strengthen the city economy. Here is what we found.

Projections: The City in 1985

In a companion volume, George Sternlieb and James Hughes estimate the city's probable population and work force in 1985. Their forecasts show a loss of 300,000 jobs between 1975 and 1985, with more than half of the decrease attributable to drops in government employment. By 1985, they say, total employment will stabilize at about 3.2 million jobs.

One major result of the projected job loss will be a reduced 1985 city population. It will, according to Sternlieb and Hughes, approach 7.2 million, compared to 7.5 million in 1975, 7.9 million in 1970. A large portion of this projected 1985 population -- about 2.8

million people -- will be between 25 to 44 years of age. The number of people below 14 years and above 45 years of age will decrease significantly from their current percentage of the total population.

To the degree that one believes that numerical declines in jobs and population translate into qualitative declines in the life and economy of a city, then some of the Sternlieb-Hughes projections may be characterized as "pessimistic," while others may be open to differing interpretations. For example, the decrease in the overall city population includes a substantial growth in the 25 to 44 year old age group. This is usually the period when most people are at their peak in productivity, including their earning and spending power. That, it seems to us, is a favorable sign for the city.

However one regards their projections, the authors make it clear that most of their numbers are "future expectations" and not an "unconstrained forecast." There is room to alter at least some of the conditions or trends upon which the projections are based. These opportunities include the economic and housing programs which the city stresses in the years ahead.

One area where the city has virtually no control are changes in values toward marriage and family. A strong trend toward smaller households figures heavily in the Sternlieb-Hughes projections for 1985, and they see this as linked to a national change in the size and character of the American household. What this means for New York is major growth in the number of single family households and the households composed of two or more unrelated adults.

This boom in small households produces paradox. While the city population may shrink to as low as 7.2 million people by 1985, the number of households will actually increase. Sternlieb and Hughes say that between 1975 and 1985 the number of households will rise from 2.86 million to more than three million. Not surprisingly, this increase will occur largely within that same age cohort whose percentage of total population will also increase -- the 25 to 44 year olds.

The Suburbs: Potential for Inmigration

A great deal has been written, and claimed, about the potential for suburban inmigration to the nation's urban centers in the years ahead. Some cities, notably

Baltimore and Seattle, have mounted major campaigns to retreive their suburban middle-class populations. How many suburban commuters can New York City tap for city residency?

With the exception of some separated, widowed or divorced suburbanites, whose estimated numbers are included in the Sternlieb-Hughes projections, there seem to be severe limits on the number of suburban households, headed by husbands and wives, who can be induced to live in New York City in the years ahead.

Kristina Ford's work on this question (see Chapter Four of this volume) shows that only 11 percent of 600 commuters interviewed for the study showed any inclination towards New York City living. In these cases, the contemplated move into the city is eight years away.

The commuters in the survey showed high incomes (their median annual income is $36,046), own their own homes, and have school-age children -- one of the strongest reasons they give for living in the suburbs. The education and other attractions of suburban living, such as recreation, suggest the obvious limitations of city housing policy alone as a means of capturing large numbers of suburban residents.

The 11 percent who indicate plans for a future move to New York will do so only after their children have grown. Their interests in city living are matched mainly to two of the city's major housing types -- high rise apartments (predominantly in Manhattan) or the purchase of a town house or brownstone.

Recent City Housing Programs

Both the city and the state have in the past launched and sustained major housing programs aimed at retaining New York City's middle-class population. Keeping these families in the city has certainly been one rationale for rent control, as it also has been for Mitchell-Lama housing.

The city and state have also built or planned large-scale housing developments on a "new town" scale to offer an alternative to the suburbs. Coop City, Starrett City, the proposed Battery Park City are examples. The most recently-completed of these large-scale projects, Roosevelt Island, succeeded in capturing about 25 percent of its residents from outside of the city. The remainder were already city residents, many of whom found in the Island an opportunity to stay in New York.

But the direct and indirect costs of these efforts have been substantial. On the subject of rent control, for example, numerous studies have suggested that rent regulations, while keeping rents low for tenants, have also contributed to the erosion of the city's housing stock by restricting building income; and this, in turn, often meant deferred maintenance by owners. The Mitchell-Lama housing program is in bankruptcy. A CHPC study issued last year* estimated that the deficit between rent revenue and the costs of Mitchell-Lama housing were more than $100 million and growing by $30 million annually.

The New York State Urban Development Corporation, the sponsor of the Roosevelt Island project, is now out of the housing business due to the financial strain of its past housing programs.

The entrepreneural roles of the city and state, as bankers or developers of housing, are over for the foreseeable future. For low rent housing, it is very clear that the federal government will have to provide the development incentives through conventional public housing or through Section 8 combined with FHA insurance.

For the city's projected work force -- the middle income and above families, including the smaller households projected by Sternlieb and Hughes -- the city may have to provide indirect, albeit critical, boosts for the housing types that will attract or retain them. What kind of housing will that be?

Current City Housing Programs

This study dwells on housing created by two city tax subsidies: the J-51 tax exemption and abatement, which since 1975 has been extended to include the conversion of manufacturing, loft and commercial space into residential use; and the 421 tax incentives, which provides a temporary, but substantial, abatement on property taxes for both rehabilitation and new construction. These two programs have stimulated virtually all of the recent

---

*Muchnick, David. Financial Realities in Publicly Assisted Housing, Citizens Housing and Planning Council of New York, 1977.

housing rehabilitation and construction activity in New York City.

While our observations on the costs and benefits of these two programs should not be construed as an endorsement of the exact workings of J-51 and 421 -- indeed, J-51 was amended and extended during the course of the study -- it becomes very clear in Ford's findings (see Chapters 1,2,3 and 5) that much of the housing being created under the programs is retaining the work force as residents and is in fact helping to attract new residents to the city.

One example of how this occurs is offered by buildings converted to residential use under the J-51 program. As part of the study, 502 units in 52 recycled buildings were surveyed in the Greenwich Village, SoHo, NoHo, Chelsea and Grammercy Park areas of Manhattan. The results showed how this kind of housing is tapping and reinforcing some of the favorable trends that are part of the Sternlieb-Hughes projections.

More than half of the interviewed residents were between the ages of 20 and 40, were represented in small households, and their median income was $21,783, as opposed to a citywide median of $9,724. The relatively high incomes were explained by their occupations -- more than 50 percent were employed in managerial, professional and technical positions, compared to just over 20 percent holding such jobs in the total city population.

Resident satisfaction was extremely high. Eighty-one percent said they would move there again. The net per unit cost to the city was $6,610 in tax revenues not received as a result of J-51 benefits. However, in many cases the buildings before conversions were largely vacant and were not paying taxes to begin with. And finally, more than 30 percent of the residents we interviewed had moved to their converted apartments from addresses outside New York City. One could conclude, as CHPC has, that the J-51 program represents the melding of housing policy with economic development objectives, and that the general form, if not the specific details of the J-51 housing stimulus, should be continued.

The universe of housing being created by both the J-51 and 421 tax programs is much wider and more diverse than just converted dwellings. It also includes new high rise rental buildings as well as garden apartments in all five boroughs. Some of the products, as the reader will see, work better than others in terms of the objectives of this study. But one form of housing that should be highlighted for its economic benefit is the loft conversion created by or offered for cooperative ownership. The occupants of coop lofts emerge as the most committed to living and working in New York City. They are drawn to loft living by the ample space, the chance to customize it, and the opportunity for home ownership.

It is ironic that the loft cooperative, one of the most successful forms of new housing, has up to now proceeded in large measure without the city's help or regulation. Most of them are, in fact, illegal. And only since 1975, under the J-51 program, has legal and regulated loft space been offered in New York in any significant numbers.

While clandestine loft conversions have meant good living space for as many as 10,000 New Yorkers, they are now causing major problems. One of them is the precarious legal and financial position of the occupants. Another is the displacement by the illegals of commercial or manufacturing tenants -- a conflict that must be resolved by the city, but really can't be until the conversion process is brought under the law. CHPC has argued that the J-51 program now offers a needed inducement for legal conversions which, in turn, means that they must proceed under the city's zoning regulations, thus offering some measure of protection for existing manufacturers.

Home Ownership

The economic advantages of ownership, which constitute a major attraction of loft cooperatives, undoubtedly applies to other forms of home ownership not examined in this study. This would include cooperative ownership of conventional apartments as well as individual ownership of single family homes. Pending further study of what is happening in these sectors of the city's housing stock, we have to rely largely on anecdotal data. These suggest that the market, including the one and two person household market, is strong for these housing types in many areas of the city.

The prospect that a larger percentage of the city's population will be represented by small households does not mean an abandonment of the American tradition of home ownership and its replacement by a pattern of lonely people renting bleak warrens in high rise towers. Our survey results, plus market experience, suggest that regardless of changing lifestyles there is a strong trend, restricted only by income, towards home ownership. This trend needs to be examined much more closely in New York City, and public agencies must determine how their actions and policies can strengthen it. This would include, for example, developing policies to preserve neighborhoods of predominantly single family dwellings. Compared to suburban areas, this type of city neighborhood offers comparable housing at lower prices and can be a magnet for the existing and projected work force.

Getting Back to Basics

New York City and State have in the past mounted ambitious, even heroic, efforts to build and finance housing. For obvious reasons, those days are over. Government capacity in the housing field is more restricted. Harder choices must be made.

The bulk of the limited money available to finance and build housing, virtually all of which is federal, must be directed to the area of greatest need -- housing for families of poor or moderate income. For the middle-class and above families, whose presence and contributions to the city are critical, governmental programs will have to be more indirect. This means providing incentives for investment in housing, not unlike the incentives provided for commerce and industry. The purpose is the same and it is, in fact, mutually re-enforcing -- stimulating and improving the city economy.

The techniques include tax incentives and improvements in supporting municipal services and facilities. We have examined two of the major tax incentive housing programs and find that generally speaking they are providing the kind of housing that is stimulating the city economy. We have identified the kinds of households that will be living here in the years ahead and the targets of opportunity, as well as need, for city housing policy to retain a large percentage of the work force as residents.

The basic message in these observations and findings is that it is time for the city to get back to basics in housing policy. This means concentrating on the traditional and accepted city role of using its tax powers, its service delivery, and its municipal improvement expenditures to encourage good market forces and discourage the bad ones.

Allan R. Talbot, Executive Director
Citizens Housing & Planning Council of New York, Inc.
New York, New York

Acknowledgments

This book is the product of the combined efforts and support of many individuals. Dr. Sternlieb was a continuous source of guidance, and must be thanked for his intellectual generosity. The proposed study was encouraged and advocated by Marian Sameth and Allan Talbot, Directors of the Citizens Housing and Planning Council of New York. Austin Laber, President of the Citizens Housing and Planning Council and chairman of the Council's committee to review the progress of the study, was a very helpful critic. Steven Faust provided important aid in developing the samples. Lou Winnick, Al Walsh, Ed Potter and David Gardner were also members of the Council's committee and offered thoughtful advice. Financial support for the study was provided by the Rockefeller Brothers Fund, the New York State Division of Housing and Community Renewal, and the Ford Foundation.

Much of the credit for completion of a research effort of this magnitude must go to those who gathered the data. Particularly helpful was Kenneth Bleakly, Jr., who directed the survey of the residents of Section 421 buildings, and who analyzed the results of this survey. His analysis and knowledge of the Section 421 tax subsidy program were the foundation for Chapter 2. I need also to thank the many people who conducted the interviews. Their dedication was steadfast and overcame resistant tenants, doormen, and building supervisors. The several hundred people who were interviewed deserve special appreciation for their willingness to answer what must have seemed to be a bewildering number of questions.

I would also like to acknowledge the efforts of Bill Dolphin, the Center's computer analyst; Natalie Borisovets, the Center's librarian; Frank Gradilone, who is responsible for the graphics in the text; and Dan Sohmer, the publications director, who guided the production of this volume. Mary Picarella, whose official title of administrative assistant does not begin to describe her role, once again smoothed the many details of fulfilling a contract. Finally, particularly cordial thanks are given to Joan Frantz, Anne Hummel, and Lydia Lombardi for their heroic efforts to type manuscripts in time for stringent deadlines. Any errors that are found in the manuscript are of course the responsibility of the author.

K. F.

Introduction

The ecology of cities, both in growth and decline, is still very much a mystery. We know very little of the dynamics of vigor or the challenges of stability, and yet we are now feverishly grasping for an understanding of the processes of urban diminution.

Few of our major municipalities were planned at their inception - and even those few have matured much more as a result of broad societal interactions than of premeditation; the American city is the reflection of market forces rather than of foresight. The governance of municipalities, and the choices made among policy options have been more a reflection of short-range temporal expediencies than of contemplative wisdom.

Local governments caught in a ruthless vise of increased needs for social services and a limited tax base have begun in the last several years to analyze the costs and benefits of policies, and to gauge impacts in long time frames. Heretofore, policy parameters have been shaped by short-range opportunism, by the pressures and potentials of the moment such as the need to seize fleeting intergovernmental transfer subsidies.

The decline of cities as manufacturing centers has come so suddenly, and though more than a generation in the making, the outflow of the middle-class and their replacement by the poor has had so abrupt an impact as to bankrupt our conceptual storehouse. Once cities got started on a downward slide, losing jobs and affluent citizens, the needs of dealing with daily problems became so exigent as to preclude longer term strategic analysis.

Slowly, however, the necessity has become clear for a reconceptualization of the role and necessities of large-scale cities if they are to survive. Spurred by the increasing inflation in suburban housing costs, as well as the changing demographic pattern of the American household, the potential for retaining the more affluent residents and even reattracting suburbanites to selected central cores has taken on new luster.

Cities that are composed solely of poor people are terribly limited in the types of jobs and entrepreneurial activity which they will permit; their principal sources of income are largely confined to receipts of transfer payments, to doles from other levels of government. The opportunities they provide for their inhabitants therefore, are severely circumscribed. If, on the other hand, cities can secure residents with ample buying power and the skills which attract new industry and new jobs, they can maintain their independence as economic entities.

The diagnosis of an adversary relationship existing between rich and poor within cities is substantially fallacious. If the poor are to secure the means of bettering their status, if bridges are to be provided to middle class roles, then the presence of the more affluent is required to create a healthy business climate. If a city is to have an independent income which permits it to provide a unique and attractive variety of specialized services, it requires a tax base of substance. And a sturdy tax base is founded largely upon the presence of the affluent.

JOBS AND PEOPLE IN NEW YORK CITY[1]

After a decade (1960 to 1970) of virtual stability, New York City's economic and demographic characteristics were altered in ways without parallel in the previous half century. The post-1970 changes were so rapid that the conventional wisdom and expectations borne through the 1960s were of limited utility, and the city's linkage to a long term transformation in the nation's social and economic dynamics came into definition. No longer were the events in New York interpreted within a framework of urban-suburban competition; increasingly invoked for explanation were the realities of regional shifts, the rise of nonmetropolitan "exurban" territories, the decline of whole metropolitan areas, the exportation of labor intensive economic activities to lower cost foreign areas, and the burgeoning manufacturing role of less developed countries. Yet, even though the frame of reference has broadened, the effect on New York City may be only the result of an acceleration of forces previously at work. Indeed, despite the outward signs of stability, the city was a victim of the throes of change throughout the decade of the 1960s.

1. Between 1960 and 1970, the city's total population fluctuated in the vicinity of 7.9 million people, while its employment base continually registered about 4.0 million jobs.

2. Internally, however, rapid change was manifest. The city lost almost one-half million people through migration, the consequence of the loss of 900,000 whites and the inflow of 400,000 nonwhites. The magnitude of net natural increase (births minus deaths) barely counterbalanced the migration losses. Nonwhites increased their proportional share of the city's population from 14.7 percent in 1960 to 23.4 percent by 1970. And while the city's population experienced considerable losses among the more mature age sectors (25 to 64 years-of-age), the surging baby boom generation

(15 to 24 years-of-age) was the locus of growth.

3. Within the economic sector, the stable total job count was maintained through processes of substitution. The loss of 200,000 manufacturing jobs was compensated by increases in white collar employment - particularly in information-dependent and communications-intensive activities. The broader post industrial transformation effected a relatively smooth transition in the city's economic structure.

The alteration of society's course in the post-1970 period did not completely blunt the long term trends. However, the intersection of national shifts with the city's historic momentum generated a series of painful adjustments. No longer was the process of change one of substitution and compensation - shrinkage and contraction began to characterize the New York environment.

1. The city's population was reduced to 7.5 million between 1970 and 1975. The decline in the national rate of fertility since 1957 was replicated in New York City and net natural increases were no longer sufficient to counter the effects of outmigration. The city's outmigration approached 600,000 people over this five-year span; the net natural increase of approximately 200,000 individuals was insufficient to prevent significant population decline. We estimate the nonwhite populace to be more than 31 percent of the city's total in 1975.

2. As in the previous decade, the losses centered about the more mature age sectors of the city. Additionally, the baby bust generation - those born in the period of fertility rate declines - began to reinforce the dynamics of contraction as it matured into the 5 to 14 years-of-age category. The aging baby boom cohorts, who were found mainly in the 25 to 34 years-of-age sector, persisted as a growth locus.

3. The city's economy over the 1970 to 1975 period underwent a process of change similar

> to that of its population, as it experienced a faltering of the growth elements which historically had ameliorated the impact of declining sectors. Within five years, New York lost 500,000 jobs, the bulk of which were in manufacturing - an extension of past trendlines. Moreover, white collar employment not only failed to compensate for these losses, it also contributed to the matrix of decline. The benefits of the post industrial service transformation tended to bypass the city, accruing mainly to the newer growth poles in the southern rimlands of the nation.

As we look to the future, it is the confluence of broader national forces with the momentum of the city's past that will determine the outlines of New York as an employment and residential nexus. In the companion volume to this study, we have projected the structure and composition of New York City's population, households, and employment through the year 1985, giving regard to each of the preceding factors. Operationally, a linked economic-demographic projection model has been designed, centering about sequential cohort component analyses. In this model, population change is a function of net natural increase and migration. The former component is predicated on the city's population profile in 1970, partitioned by age, color, and sex, and aged using survival rates through three five-year periods. For each time interval, the employment projection provides the basis for determining migration, which is then used to modify the population distribution at the end of each period. The major assumption is that employment opportunity, or the lack thereof, is a principal determinant of population movements. At the end of each five-year projection interval, after the aged population is adjusted for migration, births are estimated to establish the final population levels. The latter are derived as a function of projected national fertility patterns. The employment projections, derived from a separate submodel, show a substantial diminution of the rate of decline that has characterized the recent past.

1. *Total employment in New York City is expected to stabilize at 3.2 million jobs by 1985, a loss of 300,000 jobs over the 1975 to 1985 period. The bulk of the losses will occur in the latter half of the 1970s.*

2. *Significantly, government employment, which bulwarked the city's economy throughout the 1960s, is projected to account for over one-half of the job losses. Absent the fiscal crisis, New York City's employment would stabilize at a somewhat higher level.*

3. *The employment losses translate into substantial negative migration flows. The mismatch between the supply of labor and that required by the economic base generates a net outmigration of over 800,000 people from New York between 1975 and 1985.*

The population change projected for the city follows a pattern analogous to that of employment - continued contraction in size but at a rate much abated from that of the 1970 to 1975 period.

1. *The population of New York in 1985 will approach 7.2 million people, down from about 7.5 million in 1975 and 7.9 million in 1970.*

2. *With reduced levels of fertility, the gains secured through net natural increase are not sufficient to counteract the effects of outmigration.*

3. *Outmigration will be a persistent dilemma for the foreseeable future, even if employment were to stabilize immediately. During each projection interval, despite a base population depleted through the migration of the preceding period, the natural aging of the population results in an increasing number of individuals in their working-age years. As the potential supply of labor keeps exceeding the labor force demand, further impetus to outmigration is sustained.*

4. *While labor force pressures are conventionally conceived as being eased by the coming of age of the baby bust cohorts, the total size of the labor force will continue to increase, at least through 1985. While the number of new entrants will certainly decrease, their absolute magnitude is greater than that of the older cohorts leaving the labor force.*

5. *At the same time, nonwhites are projected to represent 50 percent of the city's total population by 1985, a consequence both of white outmigration and the lower fertility rates of whites.*

6. *The great bulk of the population in 1985 - 2.8 million out of 7.2 million people - will be concentrated in the 25 to 44 years-of-age sectors, into which the baby boom cohorts will have matured. The number of individuals below 14 years-of-age and above 45 years-of-age will contract significantly.*

The city will have lost over 660,000 people between 1970 and 1985, but many of the consequences of population decline will be mitigated by the city's linkage to another national transformation - the changing size and configuration of America's household.

1. *Nationally, primary individual households - singles or two or more unrelated individuals - are the fastest growing living arrangement; traditional husband-wife families the slowest.*

2. *Reflecting this development, as well as that of declining rates of fertility, is the long term shrinkage in size of the American household. A surge in household formations has been projected nationally. Between 1975 and 1985 the number of households is expected to increase by almost one-quarter.*

3. *New York City has been at the frontier of this evolution, evidencing households consistently smaller than those of the rest of the nation, and markedly skewed toward "atypical" households.*

4. *As these tendencies persist in the future, our projections indicate considerable growth in the number of households and in housing demand in New York City. Despite continued population declines, the city will secure over 200,000 additional households between 1975 and 1985, an increase from 2.86 million to over 3 million households.*

5. *Virtually all of these gains in the number of households are accounted for by the baby boom generation - the bulk of the additional household heads will be between 25 and 44 years-of-age. And the emerging formats will be dominated by primary individual households. As a result, the demand for housing will not abate, but will increase, even as the total population undergoes a long term decline.*

These projections must be viewed as a series of future expectations based upon very specific conditions and assumptions; they are not to be considered unconstrained forecasts. They will reflect future reality only to the degree that the linkages and relationships we have specified remain valid and operative over the next decade. Consequently, our projections represent one possible developmental track of New York City's continuing economic and demographic evolution. The overall study defines a set of future parameters - a number of leverage points - giving the city an opportunity to alter the projected course of events. At the same time, however, some of the forces and trends in effect are of such fixed momentum and inertia as to be virtually immune to deflection. Consequently, the basic tendencies that are projected are probably correct in pattern and direction; their precise scale and magnitude are subject to somewhat more uncertainty. A full description of the findings is found in the companion volume of this study.

MIDDLE CLASS HOUSING SUBSIDIES IN NEW YORK CITY

There is an enormous capacity for public policy in New York City to alter its future. The data and projections briefly presented above with regard to jobs and populations through 1985 are not immutable. They represent the shape of past realities and a view of the future assuming no major intervention or extraordinary national or local change.

The vision they give is one in which the population decline of New York City is much abated. This is paralleled by a bottoming out of the job losses which dominated the early seventies. Both of these elements are strongly conditioned on the continued vigor and growth of the service sectors and of the finance, insurance, and real estate enterprises particularly. While the city's population loss is projected to be approximately a quarter of a million individuals between 1975 and 1985, the distribution by age sector indicates that a greater proportion of the city's residents will be within the prime working years, and that there will be a relative decline in the number of dependents. By 1985, there will be 300,000 more New Yorkers between 25 and 34 years-of-age than a decade before; the number between 35 and 44 years will increase by approximately 400,000. Simultaneously, the schooling burdens will be much reduced with a decline of 300,000 individuals who are aged 5 to 14 years. In turn, these numbers lead to a dominance of a new household type, one that is relatively youthful, relatively affluent, and that has few children. Indeed, the number of households projected for 1985 is about 200,000 more than were found in 1975.

The challenge of providing jobs to this augmented labor force should not be underestimated. However, the promise of less need for human services at both ends of the age spectrum, and of a greater proportion of income available for current expenditures is evident. More than a third of the households in 1985 will be made up of primary individuals with husband/wife primary families actually representing less than half of the total within the city. These are developments which parallel the national trend lines, though they are accentuated in New York.

Housing policy is an essential weapon in the city's struggle to maintain and perpetuate itself, to provide an attractive living environment which enhances the accomplishments and aspirations of its inhabitants, which provides a tax base and a business environment that will sustain and increase the chances of meaningful livelihood for all of its people.

There are strong new tides at work both on the national scene and within the city itself which have great promise. While the fiscal crisis is far from resolved, the increased flow of federal and state funding provides a base for stabilizing the local tax rates while enhancing service delivery. For example, recent federal initiatives and policy statements regarding the location of new federal facilities give some promise that the decline in the number of public sector jobs within the city may be abated.

The city's capacity to hold its higher income groups and to provide an environment in which residents can secure income increments equivalent to national increases has diminished over time. For example, all New York City's renters had a median income of $5,500 in 1965. The U.S. total for families and primary individuals at that time was $5,862. By 1975, the equivalents were $8,395 in New York, but $11,101 for the nation's families and primary individuals.[2]

In order to remain an independent economic entity, New York City must successfully compete for those enterprises that are principals in the new post industrial growth. Key to this are housing programs which attract and keep the relatively affluent individuals who possess the specialized skills and talents which are essential to the city's future role. Middle-class housing will complement the communications/information/production service activities of the future.

The housing programs which are considered in this study provide shelter for relatively affluent people. Indeed, $15,000 per annum could be considered the minimum income required by the typical beneficiary of the two programs, the J-51 conversion program and the Section 421 new housing subsidy. This yearly income is enjoyed by barely a fifth of the city's total renter households. But the fact of these forms of subsidy largely being limited to households in higher income brackets should not deny their importance to the city as a whole.

One of the functions of the work which follows is to define the total municipal cost/benefit secured from the facilities which are generated by the programs. Again, let us stress that this is not to demean the importance of other forms of subsidy for individuals with lower incomes. However, given the limited level of municipal funding which is available, housing for poorer citizens must be supported by state and federal mechanisms. A very important step in this direction has been the increasing use of the Section 8 program. A major research effort is presently underway, outside of this presentation, to define the levels of coverage which are being provided. Similarly, under a variety of hybrid mechanisms, there are a host of rehabilitation efforts intended to extend the life and improve the quality of the city's extant housing. The sum of these efforts is gradually being felt in a significant upgrading of much of the city's shelter stock. (See Appendix A for a partial list of rehabilitation programs in New York City.)

There is a very harsh reality which dominates the housing scene and which cannot be avoided. Bluntly, new housing for anybody other than the most affluent cannot be provided without significant subsidies. The scale of these required subsidies would beggar the municipal treasury. New York has on many occasions attempted to provide housing by itself, as in the present levels of subsidy attached to Mitchell-Lama housing or the Municipal Loan Program for rehabilitation. *However, deep subsidy programs in the future must be borne by federal support because they defy in all but selected settings the city's capacities.*

How is middle class housing to be encouraged? What are the costs and fiscal benefits of measures to reinforce the city's role as a place of residence for affluent individuals? This study is offered as an effort to resolve, at least in part, these important questions. It focuses on two forms of middle class subsidy which have been developed to a considerable level of sophistication within New York City.

The first of these supports the conversion of nonresidential structures to housing. The loss of manufacturing and much of the jobbing activity which once dominated New York's employment has left behind a variety of structures for which there is little commercial demand. And these are only part of the structural stock which is open to recycling. A major additional resource, for example, is the older, no longer marketable hotels which dot the city. While unofficial conversion of such facilities for relatively unorthodox residential purposes (the artist's atelier for example) certainly predates our century, it is only within the last half dozen years that such efforts have been undertaken on a very broad basis. In New York City, they have been encouraged by the J-51 tax benefits program (see Chapters 1 and 5 for a full description of the program). This provides a substantial tax reduction not only for the costs of rehabilitation, but also for current real estate taxes on the converted property.

The second program involves the subsidization through tax abatement of new residential construction within New York - the Section 421 program. This program encourages the construction of new residential facilities under certain circumstances, with taxes for the improvement partially exempt over a finite period of time (for a full description, see Chapter 2). While initially envisioned as a program which would specifically yield lower rents in return for these abatements, the very high cost of new construction in New York City has made the program nearly essential to the provision of any new marketable apartments.

Both of these programs have been the subject of controversy. Their periodical renewal has engendered substantial debate on their merits and the advisability of their continuance. The direct costs of the programs through foregone taxes are relatively clear; the full fiscal systems impact has been largely conjectural. Are there new residents attracted to the city by the structures made possible through these programs? Or are we playing musical chairs, moving people from one form of housing within the city to another? What parts of the city's job base are filled by the individuals attracted by these two different mechanisms? What are the full tax implications of their presence? What is their spillover impact on other forms of enterprise within the municipality, for instance its restaurants and shopping facilities? Does each subsidy attract a unique part of the middle-class?

It is to these questions that our consideration is focused. The basic demographic characteristics of the households who are accommodated by each of these programs is defined based upon 1,000 interviews split evenly between the two programs. (See Chapters 1, 2 and 3.) The data in combination with appropriate municipal records and other secondary data, enable us to derive a basic cost-revenue analysis (see Chapter 5).

Finally, an additional survey was undertaken to gauge the potential movement to the city by its commuters. Because these individuals work in New York City and incur its payroll taxes and the frictions of commuting, they are targeted as being the suburban residents most likely to move to the city.

For the purposes of this study, we have taken a random probability sample of a thousand rail commuters divided appropriately between the major railroad networks that tie the city and its suburban communities in New York State, Connecticut, and New Jersey. Who are the individuals who contemplate moving back to the city? To what degree are they impacted by the new subsidy programs? What would it take to broaden the market? Chapter 4 provides the answers to these questions.

The merchandizing of cities - the mixture of appeals to be generated and their costs, the partitioning of selected targets to yield optimal returns, the provision of a package of goods and services that is affordable by the city as well as of interest to potential recipients, is an enormously demanding art form. Successful implementation of it is an absolute necessity, if the vitality of New York City is to be maintained.

George Sternlieb, Director
Center for Urban Policy Research
Rutgers University
New Brunswick, New Jersey

FOOTNOTES

1. This section of the introduction is a summary of the work that can be found in the companion volume to this study, entitled Jobs and People: New York City, 1985, by George Sternlieb and James W. Hughes.

2. George Sternlieb and James W. Hughes, Housing and Economic Reality: New York City, 1976. (New Brunswick, N.J.: Center for Urban Policy Research), p. 102.

A Section 421 apartment building typical of the high-rise, modern structures that have been constructed in Manhattan.

Frank Gradilone

Frank Gradilone

A recycled building that was once occupied by commercial tenants and that has been converted for residential use.

Housing Policy & the Urban Middle Class

Chapter 1

CONVERTED BUILDINGS

INTRODUCTION

The conversion of commercial and industrial space to residential use is a strong and important movement in New York City, a movement that could provide the city with new housing units as it simultaneously finds a use for vacant space in declining manufacturing districts. The movement has almost exclusively been illegal, which means that the conversions have taken place in buildings located in zones which do not allow residential use, or that the conversions do not conform to the New York City Building Code or to the standards of the Multiple Dwelling Law. The attraction of conversions of commercial buildings is most apparent from the willingness of people to spend a substantial amount of money on space that they have no legal right to occupy and from which they can be summarily evicted. For those who choose to convert units legally, New York City offers a tax benefits program (described in detail later) to encourage more legal conversions.

Offering tax benefits to encourage conversions takes into account competing viewpoints. The side which favors the city's facilitating conversions argues merits on several grounds. First, although residents who convert space illegally spend a large amount of money, they are typically more concerned with cosmetic changes than they are with meeting city standards for such alterations as new wiring. It could well be that the illegal conversions will have a shorter economic life than conversions which meet city standards. By encouraging the conversions to be legal, the city has an opportunity to be sure that safety standards are met, and perhaps of equal importance, it can be sure that a building is converted in such a way that its economic life will be extended for a long period.

Second, there are many warehouses, hotels, and office buildings that are substantially or completely vacant. The vacancies can result in present or prospective tax revenue delinquencies or reductions, and in neglect or abandonment of whole structures. In turn, the neglected or abandoned buildings have an adverse effect on neighboring commercial uses and thus further reduce tax receipts. Encouraging landlords to convert idle space to residential use can provide the essential economic impetus to keep buildings and tax accounts current.

Third, the blossoming of Soho as an attractive, lively neighborhood as a result of its many conversions can be interpreted as a signal of the possibilities of reviving or even generating other healthy neighborhoods in which residential and commercial uses are mingled. Encouraging conversions in these areas may produce new attractions to business and to residents either to come to New York City or to stay there.

Fourth, the cost of converting a building into residential units is much lower than the cost of constructing a new building, and this should allow lower rents to be charged. The need for additional housing units in New York City is readily documented by its low vacancy rate, particularly among the expensive, new units. Encouraging developers to convert commercial buildings will allow the addition of new, relatively cheaper units to the housing supply. Finally, the present form of city encouragement, a tax benefits program, offers exemptions from property tax and abatements of assessed levies, which means that the cost to the city is in revenues not collected rather than in money it must raise to pay developers. Given the city's financial situation, it is unlikely that it can easily raise substantial funding to assist in new construction. It could well be that at least in the near future, tax benefits for conversions are the major incentives the city can offer to increase its housing supply.

The most convincing argument against encouraging conversions is that the city will drive healthy businesses away from commercial districts because landlords will perceive a greater profit to be made from residential use than from business enterprises. It is undeniable that this would be a harmful result of residential conversion. However, there are several approaches to circumvent this result, ways that the Department of City Planning has been careful to detail and recommend forcefully in its proposals for zoning changes to allow conversions.[1] Buildings with small floor space (for instance those with less than 7500 square feet) are unlikely to attract new enterprises into spaces above the second floor because many businesses use modern manufacturing methods, such as assembly lines, which favor large spaces on one floor. The cost of moving products up and down elevators in a small building is unnecessary when suburban manufacturing districts can offer spacious buildings, or when there are buildings in the city with sufficient floor areas that a product can be assembled on a single floor. If the city zoning statutes were not to allow mixed commmercial and residential uses in the smaller buildings, the ordinances would in effect encourage vacancy or drive business away as landlords converted entire buildings to residential use. The Department of City Planning proposes allowing intra-building mixed use so that landlords can earn a profit without evicting industrial tenants.

Perhaps the most direct way to ensure that the city does not encourage business to leave is to encourage it to stay. The city planners recognize this simple equation, and propose an incentive similar to the residential tax benefits program. This incentive would help firms that are considering moving into new suburban buildings to consider instead rehabilitating their structures in the city.

This discussion has summarized the benefits to New York City that can be gotten from encouraging the conversion of commercial structures to residential use, and has shown that the city has the means to respond to the fears that business will leave precipitantly. Thus it seems that with some easily implemented provisions to protect viable commercial tenants, the city can benefit from partially sponsoring conversions. There could be structurally sound converted units, newly enlivened neighborhoods, decreased vacancies in existing structures, better maintained buildings, and an increased housing supply.

The conversion of commercial and industrial buildings to residential use is of current popular interest, but except for anecdotal information to be found in newspapers, magazines, or books of photographs, there is little definitive data about the units or buildings converted, about the neighborhoods where conversions occur, or about the people who live in the recycled buildings. A study of residents of converted units that was completed in October, 1977, offers detailed information about the conversion movement and who has been involved with it. This study found out the physical and financial characteristics of converted units as well as personal and attitudinal characteristics of the residents of conversions. This chapter will describe these characteristics and answer questions about the attractions of converted space, the advantages and penalties of living in converted units, the desires and satisfactions of residents, and how important the amenities of living in converted space have been for inducing the residents to remain in New York City. A description of the methodology of the research can be found in Appendix B.

This chapter is divided into four parts. The first discusses characteristics of converted buildings and the units to be found in them, and includes a differentiation between legal and illegal conversions. The second part describes the characteristics of the neighborhoods in which recycled buildings are found. The third part presents profiles of the residents of converted buildings; and the final part speaks to questions about the satisfaction of the residents of converted units, about the city services that they desire, and about the inducements to stay in New York City that these residents feel. Included in this attitudinal section is a discussion of whether the converted buildings are attracting tenants from other city-supported buildings.

PART I: CONVERTED BUILDINGS AND THE HOUSING UNITS CREATED

The phenomenon of creating or recycling residential units out of space once used as a hotel, an office building, or a warehouse, has provided people in New York City the opportunity to find unique places to live as alternatives to the more traditional housing in the city. The discussion which follows will describe the units in the recycled buildings that offer residential opportunities.

The conversion of buildings has been predominantly illegal. The recycled buildings were designed and constructed for industrial or commercial endeavors, and conversion is illegal either because the structures are in districts of the city where residential use is prohibited, or because the buildings do not meet the city standards for residential occupancy as detailed in the New York City Building Code and the Multiple Dwelling Law. However, because the conversion activity is so widespread, the city has taken some steps to facilitate it, and has twice amended its zoning law to allow recycling. It is possible now to convert legally, but only 10 percent of the residents and owners have chosen to do so. And even the conversions that are now legal are largely the results of illegal development. While this signals the strength of the demand for converted space, it could also mean that the structures converted illegally will not last as long as they would have if the work had been performed to conform to city standards. This may be reason enough to argue that the city take a more active role in encouraging conversions than it has in the past - not only will the safety of the citizens be protected, but the economic life of the buildings will be extended if conversions are made which comply with city codes.

Conversions are of two types. First is the conventionally converted space in which the owner has chosen to create fairly typical dwelling units in a one-time commercial or industrial building. In this instance, the tenant will come to a building that from the outside retains the characteristics of its former use, and that does not look like an apartment building. But once inside the converted unit, the tenant will discover a residence much like any other apartment in the city, although a few amenities such as high ceilings or large windows may be apparent, amenities which remind the resident of the building's former employment. These units, which in this report will be called converted apartments, are a new and small part of the current recycled market, and are all legal.

The second type of conversion is the unconventionally converted space, in which the owner has decided to offer dwellings to which he has done little or nothing. In the typical case, the tenants must provide necessities such as bathrooms,kitchens, or dividing walls in order to make the unit habitable. In this instance, the tenant finds not only a building with an exterior denoting its one-time use, but the residential units too are unique. This type of conversion is popularly called a residential loft, a term that this chapter will employ. The amenities of this type of conversion, which will be described below, are the ones that encouraged people to convert space illegally. For the most part, any residential lofts that are now legally occupied were developed initially as illegal uses, and later sought legal status.

A comparison of the two types of conversions will illuminate the characteristics of these newly available housing units. All the conversions are in buildings which once housed nonresidential uses, such as manufacturing plants or commercial offices, and the characteristics reported below have been compiled from the responses to interviews that were conducted with residents of conversions.

Converted Apartments

The apartments that have been recycled from a commercial building offer the tenants an average of 610 square feet. These units are found in buildings that have an average of 11 floors, and in which there are approximately 130 units. According to the respondents, 90 percent of these relatively small, converted apartment buildings are occupied, and the tenants typically pay $393 per month for rent and $33 for utilities.

People who move into these converted apartments generally need only provide decorating improvements.

Although 3 percent of the respondents who live in these units reported spending money on structural improvements, these outlays were discretionary rather than mandatory improvements such as installing sleeping lofts or modernizing a workable kitchen.

Residential Lofts

The physical characteristics of residential lofts are markedly different from converted apartments. Most notably, the average unit size is nearly 2100 square feet. Exhibit I-1 demonstrates the remarkable difference in size between the two types of converted units by showing floor plans typical of each. Only 37 percent of the residents did not have to make major structural improvements to the units, and these occupants reported that the previous tenant had installed items such as a kitchen and a bathroom. The remainder of the respondents reported spending an average of $7108 on their units for capital alterations. The buildings which contain these units have an average of 8 floors and 12 units, and the respondents reported that nearly all the units are occupied. Few of the buildings offer laundry facilities, and nearly half of them do not have improved hallways or entry ways. Tenants pay median prices of $392 for rent and $47 for utilities each month.

While nearly half of the buildings that offer residential lofts have been certified as legal for residential use, almost all were developed illegally. However, some sense of the difference between legal and illegal spaces can be gotten by comparing what is available under each status within the general category titled "residential lofts."

Illegal lofts offer an average of 2343 square feet, while legal lofts offer 1890 square feet. Thus, although the rent for each type of unconventional conversion is nearly the same when considered per unit ($393 for legal, $390 for illegal), it is quite different when considered per square foot ($.21/square foot per month for legal; $.17/square foot per month for illegal). Residents of illegal units spend 21 percent less on major improvements than do legal residents ($7863 spent by legal residents; $6248 by illegal residents).

Exhibit I-2 summarizes the characteristics of units in recycled buildings, and shows the great difference between converted apartments and residential lofts.

EXHIBIT I-1

FLOOR PLANS TYPICAL OF CONVERTED BUILDINGS

Typical Residential Lofts

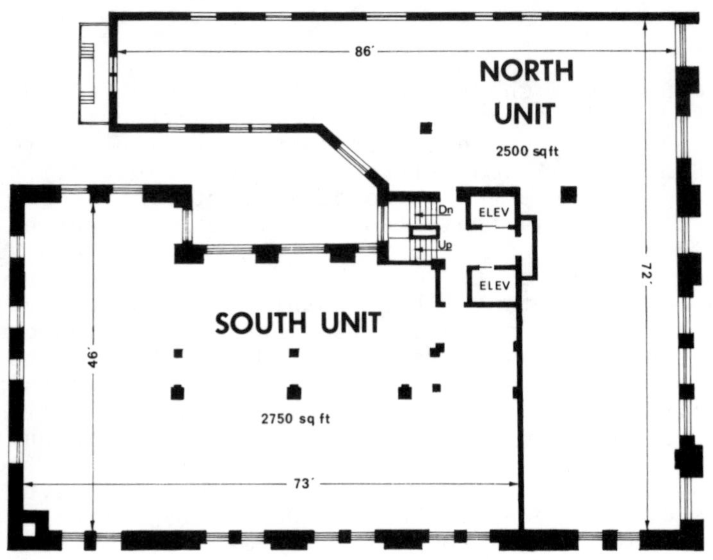

Typical Converted Apartment

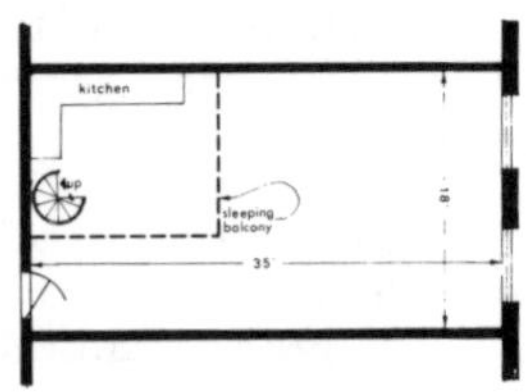

EXHIBIT I-2

CHARACTERISTICS OF UNITS IN CONVERTED BUILDINGS

	CONVERTED APARTMENTS	RESIDENTIAL LOFTS		
		All Units	*Legal*[1]	*Illegal*[1]
Building Characteristics				
Floors	11	8	*8*	*8*
Units	131	12	*12*	*11*
Percent Occupancy	89%	98%	*100%*	*94%*
Improved Entranceway	91%	58%	*62%*	*54%*
Improved Hallways	82%	56%	*59%*	*53%*
Laundry Facilities	100%	23%	*22%*	*24%*
Unit Characteristics				
Completely finished units	98%	37%	*48%*	*22%*
Money spent on improvements[2]	0	$7,108	*$7,863*	*$6,248*
Time spent on improvements: percentage who reported spending at least 6 months	0%	45%	*49%*	*42%*
Unit size	610 sq.ft.	2,090 sq.ft.	*1,887 sq.ft.*	*2,343 sq.ft.*
Number of windows	3	9	*8*	*10*
Rent Paid Per Month				
Per Unit	$393	$392	*$393*	*$390*
Per Square Foot	$.64	$.19	*$.21*	*$.17*

Notes: [1]These are categories within the general rubric "Residential Lofts."
[2]Five respondents reported spending $1,000, but this was to replace workable kitchens.

Source: CUPR Survey of Residents of Converted Buildings, August-September, 1977.

Within the category of lofts can be found the differences between legal and illegal units, of which the most striking are the rents paid per square foot. Perhaps the most remarkable fact on the exhibit is the amount of money that tenants have spent on units to which they have no legal claim. This has a dual implication that tenants do not think it likely that the city will make them leave, and that the space and other amenities available in the lofts make worthwhile the risk of losing the money spent on improvements.

Attractions and Detriments of Recycled Dwellings

All the respondents were asked what it was that attracted them the most to their unit originally, and also what they find most attractive after living there for some time. Exhibit I-3 demonstrates the shifts in attractive features perceived by residents, and shows the differences between the two groups. Size is clearly the most important initial attraction to the lofts, and is nearly twice as important a factor for these units as it is in converted apartments. What is interesting about the responses is the marked downward shift in rating of importance for practical concerns such as price and convenience. While these are important initially, after tenants live in a unit for a time, they find that it is the uniqueness or attractiveness of the unit itself that is most important.

The respondents were asked also about what they thought was the most detrimental feature of the unit. Exhibit I-4 lists the pattern of answers, demonstrating the similarity of answers between the two groups of residents. The only important differences are the frequency that small size, noise, and "nothing," are mentioned. For the residents of lofts, the mention of small size is rare among illegal occupants, and when made by a legal resident, it usually refers to a particular room, such as the kitchen; when it is noted by residents of converted apartments, it typically refers to the entire unit. The difference in complaints about noise is principally in the source of the noise, with residents of converted apartments making the conventional complaint about their interior walls, while residents of residential lofts speak of noise from trucks much more often. And finally, a significantly higher percentage of the residents of lofts find there are no detrimental features than is true of residents of converted apartments.

EXHIBIT I-3

UNIT ATTRACTION AND SATISFACTION

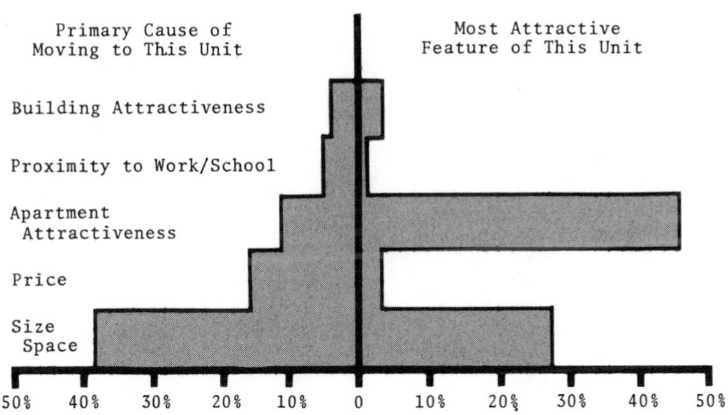

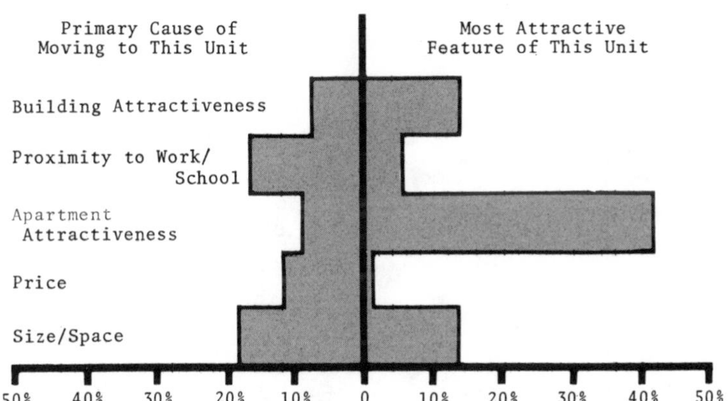

Source: CUPR Survey of Residents of Converted Buildings, August-September, 1977

EXHIBIT I-4

MOST DETRIMENTAL FEATURE OF CONVERTED UNITS

	CONVERTED APARTMENTS	RESIDENTIAL LOFTS		
		All Units	*Legal*[1]	*Illegal*[1]
Small size	15%	7%	*11%*	*2%*
Poor building services	10	12	*11*	*14*
Internal noise	10	2	*3*	*1*
Price	6	5	*7*	*2*
Poor building maintenance	6	7	*4*	*11*
External noise	6	16	*11*	*22*
Few windows	5	3	*2*	*4*
Poor building security	3	3	*5*	*1*
Undesirable neighborhood	3	2	*1*	*3*
No neighborly contact	1	0	*0*	*0*
No private room	2	1	*1*	*1*
Being responsible for everything	1	1	*1*	*1*
Nothing	11	14	*16*	*12*
Other	21	27	*28*	*26*

Note: [1]These are categories within the general rubric "Residential Lofts."

Source: CUPR Survey of Residents of Converted Buildings, August-September, 1977.

PART II: NEIGHBORHOODS WHERE CONVERSIONS OCCUR

There are two types of neighborhoods that have commercial and industrial buildings converted to residential use; the first are areas traditionally residential, the second are locations traditionally commercial and industrial. The difference between the two areas is immediately apparent. In the first there are the typical facilities appurtenant to residential use -- schools, parks, trees, and grocery stores; in the second there are all the facilities accessory to trade -- loading docks, many trucks -- and few of those necessary to living. Drive through the trade neighborhoods on a weekend or at night and you will find the areas virtually abandoned. This section will describe and explain the neighborhood conditions and their importance to people living in converted buildings.

The neighborhoods that have traditionally been residential will be termed conventional neighborhoods in this study; the areas that traditionally have been the loci of commercial and manufacturing endeavors will be called unconventional neighborhoods. The Department of City Planning defined each neighborhood where conversions have taken place so that a representative sample could be drawn. With some exceptions, the areas that were defined as conventional neighborhoods are the Village (inclusively defined to encompass the various subsets of the Village that residents refer to, such as the West Village and the East Village) and the Midtown Central Business District. Again with some exceptions the areas that were defined as unconventional neighborhoods are Noho, Soho, Tribeca, and the Midtown Loft Area. The exceptions to these definitions are the tiny areas that have traditionally had a use different from that of the larger neighborhood. For example, an address on Greenwich Street is located in a part of the Village that has long been industrial. Appendix C provides maps and definitions of the neighborhoods being considered.

All respondents were asked to describe their neighborhoods according to the ambience of the area and to their personal sense of similarities with other residents. Residents of conventional neighborhoods reported a pleasant ambience in 78 percent of the responses; those who live in the unconventional neighborhoods reported a pleasant atmosphere 63 percent of the time.

Although these two percentages are significantly different according to statistical tests, it should be noted that a very high percentage of residents of each type of neighborhood find their area pleasant. Equal percentages of respondents in each type of neighborhood reported that for the most part, the area contained people similar to themselves, and this response was chosen 57 percent of the time.

Respondents were asked to comment on their neighborhood, and as Exhibit I-5 shows, there is little variation in the choice of answers between residents of the two types of neighborhoods. In fact, only two answers show much difference at all. Almost four times as many people in conventional neighborhoods mention convenience as a factor than do people in unconventional neighborhoods, and many more people remark on the peaceful attribute of the neighborhood at night if they live in unconventional areas. Once the trucks leave, these areas settle down to what some respondents liken to a country town. But note the overall distribution of positive versus negative comments: they are essentially the same for the two types of neighborhoods.

The residents were asked how far they had to go for necessities, and also asked to rank the importance of the proximity of these same necessities. Importance was reported on a scale from 1 to 5, on which 5 was "very important." Exhibit I-6 demonstrates the substantially greater distances traveled by people living in unconventional neighborhoods to get the necessities of life -- food, clothing, etc. -- and more importantly shows that the importance of nearness to these resources does not vary with the distance traveled for them. Although the residents of unconventional areas endure more inconvenience than the other residents, it seems that they do not have a different sense of the importance of convenience.

Respondents were asked to list the city-supplied services available in their area. Not surprisingly, the people in unconventional neighborhoods receive far fewer services than those living in more conventional areas. (People who live in illegal conversions, of course, do not have the right to city-supplied garbage collection.) What is interesting again is the importance the residents attach to the services. Using a 1 to 5 scale on which 5 is "very important," the residents give all services except recreational facilities a mean

EXHIBIT I-5

NEIGHBORHOOD CHARACTERISTICS

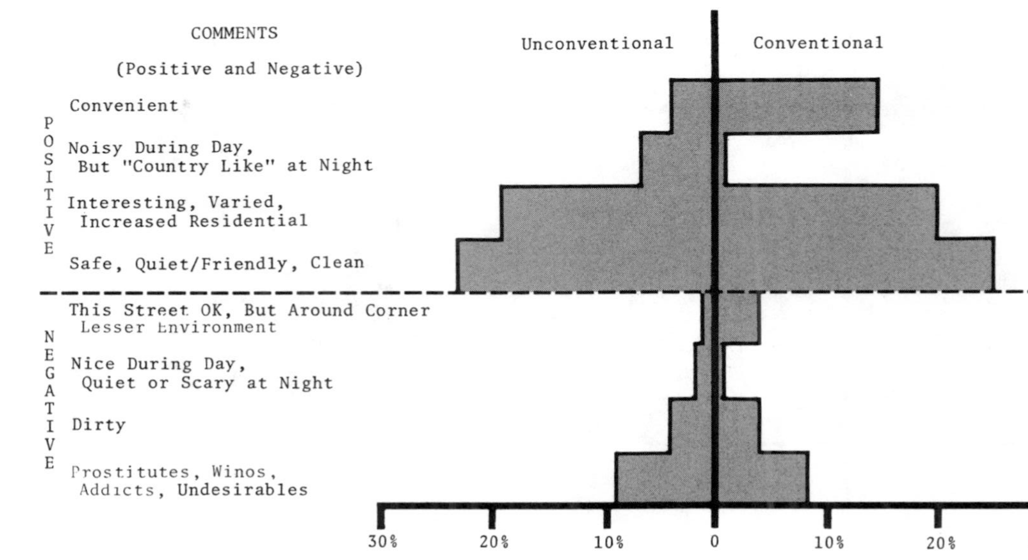

Source: CUPR Interviews of Residents of Converted Buildings, August-September, 1977.

EXHIBIT I-6

NEIGHBORHOOD CHARACTERISTICS-NECESSITIES

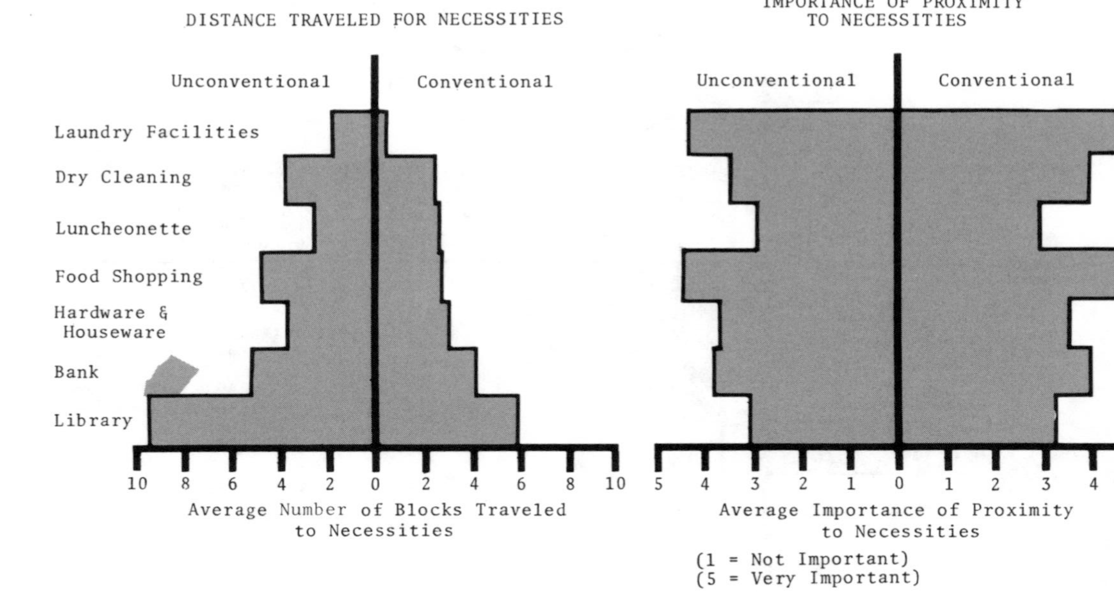

Source: CUPR Survey of Residents of Converted Buildings, August-September, 1977.

rating of 4.6, and this rating does not vary with neighborhood type. This implies that residents want the same basic city services regardless of where they live. This implication is repeated in the responses to the question, "What city-supplied services would have bettered your experience living here?" Garbage collection, street cleaning, and police protection were the most often mentioned options among residents of both types of neighborhoods. While worry about crime is a major preoccupation for many urban dwellers, the residents of the unconventional neighborhoods perceive less crime in their areas than residents of conventional areas do. This is likely to be true because there are so few people living in the unconventional areas, which means that for at least some types of crime, such as robbery or burglary, the areas do not offer many potential victims, causing would-be robbers and burglars to go elsewhere.

A final point of interest is the attractiveness of other parts of Manhattan to residents of the neighborhoods that offer converted buildings. The respondents were asked if they would like to live in each of the eight neighborhoods shown, and they could say "yes" to as many as they desired. Exhibit I-7 is a matrix which reports their answers. For example, 47 percent of the respondents now living in Tribeca would consider living in the Village. Included in the question of attraction to neighborhoods was the respondent's own neighborhood, and the percentage who said they would not live again in their own area appear as the numbers within boxes. For example, only 2 percent of the people living in the Village would not consider living there again. Overall, the Village is the most attractive area, with Soho, Noho, and Tribeca the next most alluring areas. Lower Manhattan is also appealing, probably because it is perceived as being most like Tribeca. People living in the Midtown area find the Upper East Side much more appealing than people in other neighborhoods.

Residents of converted buildings in unconventional neighborhoods stand more inconvenience and receive fewer city services than the conversion residents of more conventional areas, but their perceptions of the areas are essentially the same. And their sense of the importance of proximity to necessities is essentially the same, as is their sense of the importance of city services. The attractions of living in converted buildings have been sufficient to overcome the inconveniences associated with unconventional neighborhoods. The next part of this chapter will consider

EXHIBIT I-7

ATTRACTION TO OTHER NEIGHBORHOODS[1]

	New York City Neighborhoods[2]							
Current Residence	*Village*	*Mid-town Central Business District*	*Tri-beca*	*Soho*	*Noho*	*Mid-town Loft Area*	*Lower Man-hattan*	*Upper East Side*
Village	2%	22%	30%	65%	47%	24%	30%	38%
Mid-town Central Business District	69	28	8	39	10	50	27	61
Tribeca	47	20	2	54	31	25	62	21
Soho	48	28	67	5	64	44	48	27
Noho	56	25	50	69	15	53	47	14
Mid-town Loft Area	68	53	25	40	26	19	15	52

Notes: [1]Respondents were asked whether they would consider living in each of the eight neighborhoods shown, and could answer "yes" to as many as they desired.
[2]Appendix C reproduces a map which delineates these neighborhoods.

Source: CUPR Interviews with Residents of Converted Buildings, August-September, 1977.

the characteristics of the people who live in both types of converted buildings in both types of neighborhoods.

PART III: THE PEOPLE WHO LIVE IN CONVERTED UNITS

Thus far have been described the buildings that have been converted from a nonresidential use, the units that have been made available to tenants, and the neighborhoods where the recycled buildings can be found. In this part of the chapter will be described the people who live in the converted units. When all these residents are considered as a group, it is quickly apparent that they are quite different from other New York City citizens.

The most striking characteristics of the residents of converted buildings are their narrow range of ages, and their income, education, and profession. Over 80 percent of the respondents are between 20 and 40 years old; the median age is 31.8, significantly lower than the city median age for all renter households, which was 44.4 years in 1975.[2] And the conversion residents are very well educated, with nearly 75 percent having at least finished college. Exhibit I-8 shows how this pattern of education is nearly opposite that of New York City as a whole. The professions they pursue follow from their educated status, and a much higher percentage of these residents have jobs as professional or technical personnel, managers, or artists than is true of residents of the city as a whole. Exhibit I-9 shows the differences between the occupations of these residents and those of other New York City workers, including a comparison with the relatively specialized Manhattan workers. Finally, the household incomes are commensurate with the educational achievements, with the average being about $23,000 per year. The median household income is $21,783, over twice the city-wide median of $9,255.[3]

Other descriptive measures useful in characterizing the people living in these buildings are the sex of the head of the household, marital status, size of the household, and number of children. The surveys show that 65 percent of the heads of households in converted units are male. This is close to the city-wide figure, which shows that 66 percent of household heads are male.[4]

EXHIBIT I-8
SCHOOLING COMPLETED

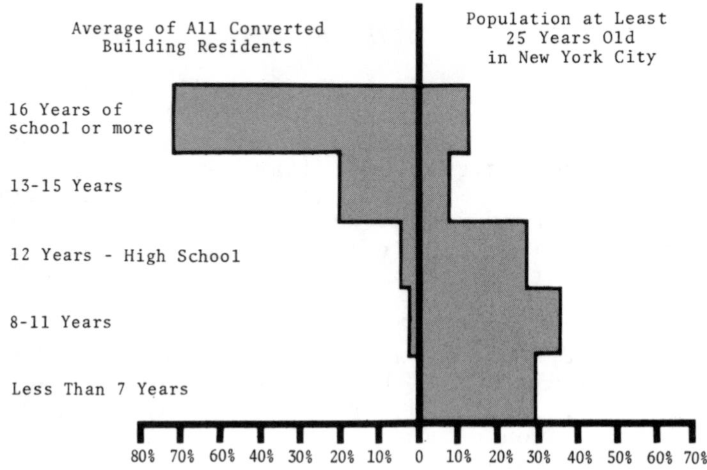

Source: CUPR Survey of Residents of Converted Buildings, August-September, 1977. U.S. Bureau of the Census, <u>Detail Population Characteristics, Part 34, New York (1970)</u>.

EXHIBIT I-9

OCCUPATIONS OF HEADS OF HOUSEHOLDS

Occupation	*Residents of Converted Buildings*	*NYC - Total (1970)*	*Manhattan (1970)*
Professional and Technical[1]	*36.0%*	13.6%	24.6%
Manager, Administrator, Proprietor	*20.2*	7.8	10.2
Sales Worker	*7.1*	7.3	7.1
Clerical	*3.1*	27.1	22.5
Craftsman, Foremen	*1.0*	10.2	5.7
Operative	*0.6*	15.0	11.6
Laborer	*0.4*	3.3	2.3
Service Worker	*4.4*	12.3	13.6
Artist	*24.3*	2.1	N/A
Other	*2.9*	1.3	2.4

Note: [1]For Manhattan, this includes artists.

Sources: U.S. Bureau of the Census, 1970 Census of Population and Housing, PHC(1)-145, Table P-401. CUPR Survey of Residents of Converted Buildings, August-September, 1977.

Over half the respondents are single and nearly a third are married; this is a different pattern from that of all renters in the city, where it is found that nearly half are married and a little more than a third are single. Nearly half of the respondents live in 2-person households, a much greater percentage than generally found in New York City (31 percent) or in Manhattan alone (28 percent).[5] Only 5 percent of the converted building residents live in households with four or more people, while for the city as a whole nearly 20 percent of the population live in such large households.[6]

As might be expected from information about household size, only 13 percent of the households have children. This implies that people with children are not attracted to these units, perhaps due to the paucity of services available to such households in unconventional neighborhoods, or perhaps simply because so few residents are married.

An important attribute of the people living in converted buildings is that nearly 33 percent of them have moved to their current unit from outside New York City, and this is a very high proportion. The most recent comparable statistic is from 1970, when only 14.1 percent of the people in the city had come from elsewhere during the previous five years. The Manhattan statistic at the same time was 21 percent, still substantially lower than was found in these new types of housing.[7] The converted buildings seem to be an attractive force.

Other factors of interest are that 56 percent of the respondents were born in New York, went to grade school in New York, went to college in New York, or experienced some combination of the three. Over half the respondents have lived in New York City more than five years, with 37 percent having been in the city more than ten years.

Given this general description of the residents, it is now useful to consider them when divided into two groups. Discussed earlier was the condition in which the units in converted buildings are presented to the market, either as raw space with at most a few facilities, or as a completely refurbished apartment. The former are called residential lofts, and the latter are termed converted apartments. All converted apartments are legal, while the lofts are occupied both legally and illegally. From the data gotten by the interviews, it is clear that the difference in the type of unit is the critical variable for differentiating among converted building residents and for understanding their attitudes toward housing.

As reported in Part 2 of this chapter, the converted apartments are small, and in most respects are similar to the standard rental unit available in New York City. Attracted to these units are largely people who are young, single, well-educated, and highly paid. The median age is 29.6 years, 64 percent of the residents are single, 69 percent have at least a college education, the median household income is $21,479, and only 7 percent of the households have children.

The residential lofts offer flexibility, large spaces, and low rent per square foot, but also require that the residents spend time and money to improve the units. Attracted to these units are people whose median age is 34 years, people with extremely high educational achievements (81 percent have at least a college degree). The median household income is $22,253; 48 percent of the residents are single, and 21 percent have children.

There are other personal factors which differentiate between residents of the two types of units. The occupations of the two groups are shown graphically in Exhibit I-10. The definitions used for these occupations follow the guidelines of the U.S. Bureau of the Census, and are listed in Appendix D. The two groups are occupied doing essentially the same things, and the preponderance of professional, technical, and managerial positions is predictable from the high educational achievements described earlier.

The only large difference between the two groups is the number of people working as artists in each. Thirty-five percent of the residents of lofts are artists, while 16 percent of residents of the more commonplace units work as artists. Although both percentages are high, the difference between them is noteworthy, and likely to be explained by the extravagant amounts of space available in lofts. These units offer an average of approximately 2100 square feet, substantially more space than the 610 square feet offered by the converted apartments. For an artist who needs a large working space, such a unit is ideal; indeed it may even be compelling because although the

EXHIBIT I-10

OCCUPATION BY CONVERSION UNIT TYPE

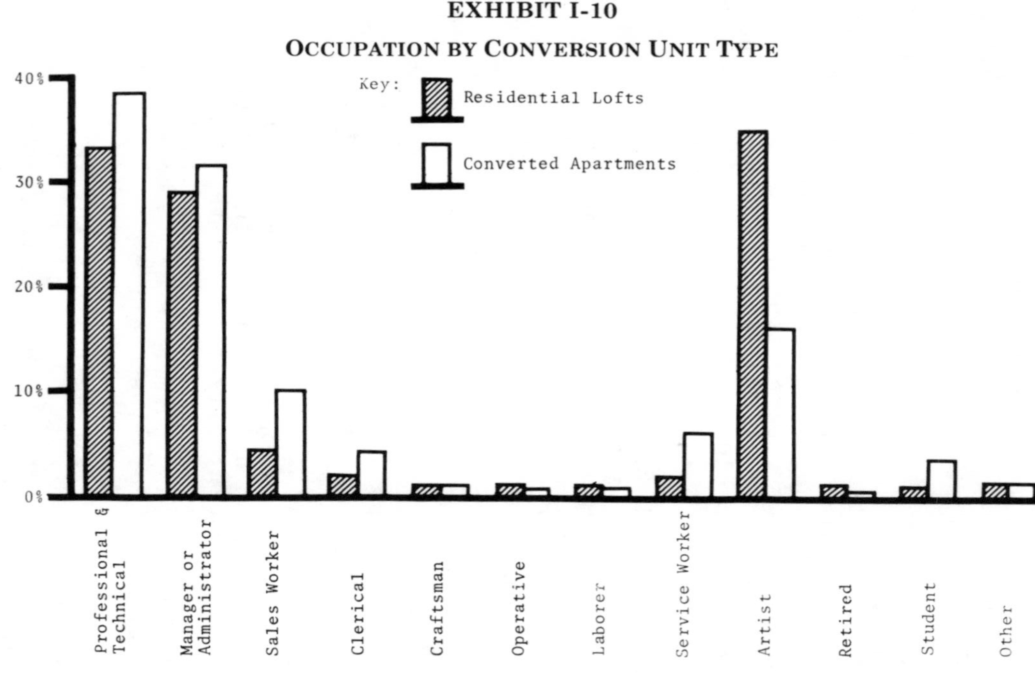

Source: CUPR Survey of Residents of Converted Buildings, August-September, 1977.

rents for the large spaces are high, the artist can combine work and living space, thereby making the total expenditure seem more readily affordable.

It was explained earlier that the large majority of residents are occupying the lofts illegally. Therefore, it is important to consider these illegal residents as a separate group. The illegal residents of the residential lofts are slightly older (median age is 34.3 years) even better educated (86.3 percent have at least graduated from college), slightly more often are married (47.3 percent are single), and earn slighly less money (median income is $19,390) than residents who legally occupy lofts. But the most striking difference between the illegal and the legal residents of conversions, and between illegal residents and all residents of New York City are the occupations that are typical of each category. Almost half of the illegal residents reported that the head of the household was an artist. This may be slightly overstated because of a sensitivity to sexual equality that was evident among residents of conversions. In response to the question, "Are you the head of the household?" many people answered that "this is a 50-50 household," presumably meaning completely shared responsibilities, and the interviewer had no choice but to consider the respondent to be the head. Thus it is conceivable that the wife of an employed man reported to us that she was an artist, and that this was included in the tally of heads of households who worked as artists. In any case, even if the percentage figure is overstated by 29 percent (the percentage of married residents living in illegal conversions), it is still shown that an extremely high percentage (31 percent in this case) of illegal residents are artists. The high percentage of artists living in illegal lofts is corroborated by the finding that in 24 percent of the illegal households there are no full time job holders. From comments the residents made, it seems that the artists supplement their incomes with part-time jobs, but in the interest of pursuing their profession do not take full time positions. Exhibit I-11 summarizes the personal and professional characteristics of residents, legal and illegal, of the two types of converted units. A fact reported on this exhibit that will be important in the next section is the percentage of each type of resident that owns the converted dwelling. While no converted apartments are owned by the residents, nearly two-thirds of the legal lofts are owned and even 8 percent of the illegal conversions

EXHIBIT I-11

PERSONAL CHARACTERISTICS OF RESIDENTS OF CONVERTED BUILDINGS

		TOTAL SAMPLE		SUB-GROUP ANALYSIS		
				Residents of Residential Lofts		
CATEGORY	NEW YORK CITY[1] Total	All Residents of Converted Buildings n = 502	Residents of Converted Apartments (All Legal) n = 278	Total n = 224	Legal n = 126	Illegal n = 98
Age of Household Head						
Less than 20 years		1.4%	1.8%	0.9%	1.6%	0%
20-29 years		41.2	50.4	29.7	31.0	27.2
30-39 years		40.4	33.9	48.4	45.2	53.3
40-49 years	N.A.	11.6	10.2	13.2	13.5	13.0
50-59 years		4.3	2.6	6.4	7.1	5.4
60 years and over		1.2	1.1	1.4	1.6	1.1
Median Age	44.4 yrs. (1975)	31.8 yrs.	29.6 yrs.	34.0 yrs.	33.8 yrs.	34.3 yrs.
Sex of Household Head	(1975)					
Male	66.3%	64.8%	62.9%	67.3%	68.0%	65.9%
Female	33.7	35.2	36.7	32.7	32.0	34.1
Marital Status of Household Head	(1970)					
Single	34.9%	56.8%	63.7%	47.9%	48.0%	47.3%
Married	49.5	32.4	27.1	39.1	38.2	40.7
(Separated)	(5.6)	(6.6)	(4.4)	(9.3)	(7.3)	(12.1)
Divorced	5.0	9.8	6.8	11.2	10.6	12.1
Widowed	10.6	1.0	0.4	1.9	3.3	0.0
Schooling Completed by Household Head	(1970)					
0-7 grades	19.6%	0.0%	0.0%	0.0%	0.0%	0.0%
8-11 grades	33.5	1.0	1.4	0.5	0.0	1.1
Completed High School	28.3	4.6	5.8	3.2	5.5	0.0
Some College or Post-High School	8.1	20.1	23.6	15.8	17.3	12.6
4 or More Years of College	10.6	74.2	69.2	80.5	77.2	86.3

(Continued)

EXHIBIT I-11 *(continued)*

PERSONAL CHARACTERISTICS OF RESIDENTS OF CONVERTED BUILDINGS

CATEGORY	NEW YORK CITY[1] Total	TOTAL SAMPLE: All Residents of Converted Buildings n = 502	SUB-GROUP ANALYSIS: Residents of Converted Apartments (All Legal) n = 278	Residents of Residential Lofts: Total n = 224	Legal n = 126	Illegal n = 98
Occupation of Household Head	(1970)					
Professional or Technical	13.6%[2]	36.0%	38.2%	33.2%	35.5%	30.3%
Artist	2.1	24.3	15.7	35.0	27.4	44.9
Manager, Administrator, Proprietor	7.8	20.2	21.3	18.7	25.0	10.1
Sales Worker	7.3	7.1	9.7	3.7	5.6	1.1
Service Worker	12.3	4.4	6.4	1.9	1.6	2.2
Clerical	27.1	3.1	3.7	2.3	1.6	3.4
Student	--	1.9	2.6	0.9	--	2.2
Craftsman, Foreman	10.2	1.0	0.7	1.4	0.8	2.2
Operative	15.0	0.6	0.4	0.9	0.8	1.1
Laborer	3.3	0.4	0.4	0.5	--	1.1
Other	1.3	1.0	0.7	1.4	1.6	1.1
Citizenship of Household Head						
United States		90.6%	90.6%	90.5%	91.5%	89.5%
Foreign	N.A.	9.4	9.4	9.5	8.5	10.5
People in the Household	(1975)					
1 person	33.7%	36.9%	42.9%	29.4%	27.0%	33.0%
2 persons	30.5	48.3	48.4	48.2	50.0	45.1
3 persons	15.2	10.8	8.1	14.2	16.7	11.0
4 or more persons	20.6	4.0	0.7	8.2	6.4	11.0
Percentage of Households with Children	N.A.	13.1%	6.8%	20.5%	22.1%	19.4%

(Continued)

EXHIBIT I-11 *(continued)*

PERSONAL CHARACTERISTICS OF RESIDENTS OF CONVERTED BUILDINGS

CATEGORY	NEW YORK CITY[1] Total	TOTAL SAMPLE: All Residents of Converted Buildings n = 502	TOTAL SAMPLE: Residents of Converted Apartments (All Legal) n = 278	SUB-GROUP ANALYSIS: Residents of Residential Lofts Total n = 224	SUB-GROUP ANALYSIS: Residents of Residential Lofts Legal n = 126	SUB-GROUP ANALYSIS: Residents of Residential Lofts Illegal n = 98
Type of Tenure	(1975)					
Own	27.5%	16.4%	--	37.2%	66.1%	8.3%
Rent	72.5	83.6	100.0%	62.8	33.9	91.7
New York City Affiliation						
Born in NYC	N.A.	39.1%	39.9%	38.2%	40.5%	35.9%
Went to Grammar School or High School in NYC		27.4	26.4	28.5	32.8	24.2
Went to College in NYC		38.4	37.4	39.1	38.2	40.0
Household Income	(1975)					
Less than $5,000	29.0%	5.4%	3.5%	7.8%	7.0%	8.9%
$5,000-$9,999	29.4	6.3	6.9	5.4	3.5	7.8
$10,000-$14,999	19.7	16.8	16.9	16.7	16.5	16.7
$15,000-$19,999 }		15.9	17.7	13.7	9.6	18.9
$20,000-$24,999 }		15.7	16.9	14.2	14.8	14.4
$25,000-29,999 }	21.9	12.9	12.3	13.7	14.8	12.2
$30,000-34,999 }		8.2	8.5	7.8	10.4	4.4
More than $35,000 }		18.8	17.3	20.6	23.5	16.7
Median	$8,395	$22,783	$21,479	$22,253	$24,526	$19,390
Full-Time Job Holders in Household						
0	N.A.	12.2%	10.9%	13.9%	6.5%	23.5%
1		53.2	58.5	46.4	49.1	43.5
2		32.8	30.2	36.1	42.6	27.1
3 or more		1.8	0.4	3.6	1.9	5.9

(Continued)

EXHIBIT I-11 *(continued)*

PERSONAL CHARACTERISTICS OF RESIDENTS OF CONVERTED BUILDINGS

Notes: [1]Where indicated, New York City figures are either for the city population as a whole, or for renter households in 1975.
[2]The category "artist," which is normally included in the totals for professional/technical workers, has been disaggregated for comparative purposes.
Numbers may not total 100.0 percent due to rounding.

Source: Center for Urban Policy Research, Rutgers University, Survey of Residents of Converted Buildings. U.S. Bureau of the Census, Detail Population Characteristics, Part 34, New York. George Sternlieb and James Hughes, Housing and Economic Reality (New Brunswick, N.J.: Center for Urban Policy Research, 1976).

are owned. (These illegal owners reported that they are filing with the city to get their lofts certified as legal.)

In sum, it can be said that living in converted buildings are a group of well-educated, affluent young people. Within this primary group of residents are two subgroups identifiable by the type of unit they have chosen to occupy, either a converted apartment or a residential loft. Somewhat older people are attracted to the latter type of unit, and often the residents are artists who need the space such a unit provides. The demographic characteristics of this part of the chapter have provided a sketch of the type of people attracted to living in recycled units, many of which having been converted illegally. The next part of the study will fill in this sketch with a portrayal of the attitudes, satisfactions, and future plans of the residents.

PART IV: SATISFACTION, INDUCEMENT, AND HOW TO ENCOURAGE IT

The interviews included several questions designed to elicit from the respondents how happy they were in their present circumstances, to ask how their satisfaction could be increased, and to determine what importance the uniqueness of their apartment has in their decision to stay in New York City. The following questions were asked during the interview.*

1. Using a scale from 1 to 5, on which 5 is very satisfied, how satisfied are you with living here?

2. Knowing what you do now, would you choose to live in a unit like this one again?

3. Would you recommend to your friends that they should live here?

4. How long do you think you will stay here?

---

*The questions were not asked at the same time; rather, they were scattered throughout the interview so that one answer would not bias the next.

5. When you move, would you live in a unit like the one you have now?

   If not, what type of unit is more appealing?

6. Before moving here, had you considered moving to the suburbs?

7. Or, had you considered more conventional housing in the city?

8. If an apartment similar to the one you live in now had not been available when you moved, would you have left the city?

9. What would you do if your rent (or maintenance fee) doubled?

By considering the answers to these several questions, the subjective view of the respondents toward living in converted buildings can be determined.

Satisfaction and How to Increase It

The direct query about satisfaction came at a point in the interview after the respondent had been asked to describe his apartment, building, and neighborhood at some length, after he had been thinking about both positive and negative aspects of his surroundings. Therefore, the responses and the patterns revealed are considered.

As much as has been remarked about the great difference between converted apartments and residential lofts, *there is no difference between the level of satisfaction of the people living in the two types of units.* Not so surprisingly, given the discussion in Part II of this chapter, there is also no difference between levels of satisfaction reported by residents of the two types of neighborhoods described earlier. And the satisfaction is high - about 4.0 on a scale which goes from 1 to 5.

Differences in satisfaction are to be found when the previous residence of the respondent is considered. People whose former residence was New York City have the highest level of satisfaction (4.1), significantly higher than that of previous foreign residents (3.4), but about the same as that reported by previous tri-state* residents (3.9), previous residents of other parts of the United States (3.8), and former residents of New York City suburbs (3.8). Perhaps the lower level of satisfaction shown by foreign residents has more to do with cultural differences than with living in New York City.

Age of the respondent has a noteworthy effect on his satisfaction, with the oldest and youngest people showing the most extreme and significant differences. Respondents who were less than 20 years old had the lowest level (3.6); while those over 60 had the highest (4.5). Respondents between 20 and 59 showed consistency among their responses, and reported levels of satisfaction between 3.9 and 4.1. Again it was the younger respondents, those between 20 and 29 years of age, who were least satisfied.

But even these differences should not obscure the overall high level of satisfaction. What is worth considering is the pattern of responses to the two-part question "What city-supplied and owner-supplied services would have bettered your experience of living in this unit?"

Residents of unconventional neighborhoods show a slightly different pattern of requests for city services to increase their satisfaction than people living in conventional areas. Although 35 percent of the residents in each type of area claim that nothing is necessary (a good corroboration of the high satisfaction ratings), nearly twice as many people in unconventional neighborhoods think better garbage collection would enhance their enjoyment than do residents in the conventional areas. This is not surprising, since in the unconventional areas it is often the case that the residents have no garbage pick-up because they are not legal occupants. They are not asking so much for better city refuse collection as they are asking for any collection at all. But the age of the respondent does not affect the pattern of requests for additional city services, nor does the place of the respondent's previous residence. The overall pattern is:

---

*The tri-state designation includes all areas of New York State, New Jersey, and Connecticut that are outside the New York City metropolitan area.

Nothing necessary	35%
Street cleaning and repairs	18
Garbage collection	14
Police/fire protection	7
Recreation facilities	6
Better public transportation	5
Better parking facilities	2
Rid neighborhood of undesirables	2
Unclassified response	11

Probably the best indicators of the validity of the high satisfaction ratings are the responses to the questions "Would you live here again?" and "Would you recommend to your friends that they live here?" Eighty-one percent of the sample say they would indeed live in the unit again, and 84 percent say they would recommend a like unit to their friends. People who live in lofts respond much more positively than even these high percentages demonstrate. This implies that although their satisfaction rating was no higher than the rating given by residents of converted apartments, in fact their contentment with lofts is higher than that of residents of the other type of conversion.

A respondent's former place of residence does not make a difference in whether or not the unit would be recommended to friends, and as many newcomers to the city would make such a recommendation as would longer term residents. However, far more people who have lived in New York City before would choose to live in their units again than would those who came from elsewhere. Particularly disenchanted are those who moved into the unit from a New York City suburb. Only 63 percent of them would choose their unit again, while 85 percent of longer-term New Yorkers would.

When those respondents who said that they would not choose their unit again, 19 percent of the total, were asked what kind of unit they would prefer, their answers show that most desirable are: any type of larger unit (25 percent), lofts (12 percent), units in renovated buildings (12 percent), or detached houses (10 percent.) The first three choices imply a predilection to stay in New York City, while a desire for a detached house probably means that the respondent wants to move to the suburbs or to an even more removed spot.

It has repeatedly been remarked in this study that the residents of converted units are largely illegal occupants. It has been suggested before that the attractions of living in the lofts have been sufficient to entice residents to invest substantial amounts of money and to endure inconvenience. A consideration of the satisfaction of this particular subset of conversion residents will show how pleased they have been with their risky decision to occupy space illegally. The level of satisfaction reported was 4.1 for illegal conversion residents, a figure not significantly higher than what was found among legal residents of converted units; and the percentage of illegal residents who would recommend a similar unit to their friends was no higher than reported for legal residents. But the percentage of illegal occupants that said they would again choose to live in the unit was higher than the proportion of legal residents of lofts. However, it should be noted that the percentages are very high - 85.5 percent for legal residents. Most people who live in converted buildings are quite satisfied, and indeed seem to find the amenities of the units sufficient to endure whatever inconvenience or insecurity they feel. Exhibit I-12 summarizes the responses to the satisfaction related questions.

Inducement

How important has the existence of units in converted buildings been to the residents' decisions to stay in the city? Several of the questions listed at the beginning of this section can help answer this difficult question. Exhibit I-13 shows the responses made by the residents, again dividing them into appropriate categories according to the type of converted unit they occupy.

The respondents were asked whether they had considered moving to the suburbs at the time they moved into their current units; if at that same time they had considered moving to a more conventional unit, i.e., a typical highrise apartment building; and finally if they would have left the city if a dwelling like the one they chose had not been available.

In the whole sample, only 14 percent of the people said they had considered moving to the suburbs - and this response does not vary by current housing type

EXHIBIT I-12

LEVELS OF SATISFACTION

INDICATOR	Whole Universe of Residents of Conversions	Type of Conversion				Place of Previous Residence[1]					Age of Respondent			Type of Neighborhood	
		Converted Apartments (All Legal)	Residential Lofts												
			Total	Legal	Illegal	NYC	NYC Metro Region	Tri-State[2]	Other U.S.	Foreign	<20	20-59	>60	Conventional	Unconventional
Satisfaction on a scale from 1 to 5, on which 5 is very satisfied	4.0	Same as Universe[3]				4.1	3.8	3.9	3.8	3.4	3.6	4.0	4.5	Same as Universe	
Respondents who would choose to live in the unit again	81.3%	74.8%	89.4%	86.5%	92.4%	85%	63%	76%	74%	74%	Same as Universe			Same as Universe	
Respondents who would recommend a similar unit to friends	83.8%	80.4%	88.2%	88.2%	88.2%	Same as Universe					Same as Universe			Same as Universe	

Notes: [1]New York City Metropolitan Region is the 22 county region as defined by the Port Authority and the Regional Plan Association, except for the five boroughs of Manhattan.
[2]Tri-State Region is New York, New Jersey, and Connecticut, except for New York City and its Metropolitan Region.
[3]"Same as Universe" means that the responses among the various subgroups were not significantly different from each other, and the responses shown in the column titled "Whole Universe of Residents of Conversions" is the appropriate response.

Source: CUPR Survey of Residents of Converted Buildings, August-September 1977.

EXHIBIT I-13

INDUCEMENT TO STAY IN NEW YORK CITY

	Whole Universe of Residents of Conversions	Converted Apartments (All Legal)	Residential Lofts			Residents With Children
			Total	Legal	Illegal	
At the time respondent decided to move into current unit						
a. Considered moving to the suburbs	13.8%	Same as Universe[1]				22.6%
b. Considered more conventional unit	55.6%	67.5%	41.4%	51.6%	28.1%	48.4%
Length of time resident plans to stay in his unit	5 yrs.	3 yrs.	8 yrs.	9.5 yrs.	6 yrs.	5 yrs.
Would have left the city if similar unit had not been available	8%	Same as Universe				15.2%
If rent or maintenance fee doubled, would leave the city	16.7%	Same as Universe				36.3%

Note: [1]"Same as Universe" means that the responses among the various subgroups were not significantly different from each other, and the response shown in the column titled "Whole Universe of Residents of Conversions" is the appropriate response.

Source: CUPR Survey of Residents of Converted Buildings, August-September, 1977.

(converted apartments or residential lofts) or by age group. However, many more people who now live in conventional neighborhoods had considered moving to the suburbs than had those now residing in unconventional areas. People whose previous residence had been suburban were nearly three times as likely to report this as an option. In spite of these differences, the low percentages seem to imply that a move to the suburbs is not a choice considered by many people who live in converted buildings.

Far fewer of the people currently living in lofts had considered living in standard apartment buildings than had those in converted apartments. However, the percentages are quite substantial: 41 percent of the people living in lofts and 68 percent of those in converted apartments had considered apartment buildings. The frequency with which people reported having thought of moving to these more traditional housing types does not correlate with the respondent's age or place of former residence.

The question about whether the respondent would have left the city if a unit similar to the current unit had not been available yielded a response that does not waver by type of unit, neighborhood, place of previous residence, or age group. Only 8 percent said yes, they would have left.

Perhaps most significant of all the findings that try to gauge inducement is the pattern of response to the question: "What would you do if your rent (or maintenance fee) doubled?" *Even considering this extreme circumstance, only 17 percent of the respondents said they would leave the city.* Perhaps by virtue of their education, their youth, their profession, certainly by virtue of their affluence, the people living in converted buildings are willing to pay even a significant increase in housing costs to stay in New York City. And the specific unit itself is not so important, as evidenced by the low proportion of people who said that they would have left the city if a similar unit had not been available.

The 13 percent of the sample that have children feel the least inducement to stay in the city, as is shown in Exhibit I-13. Significantly more of the respondents with children had considered moving to the suburbs at the time they moved into a converted building, and nearly twice the usual proportion would have left the city had a similar unit not been available. And their commitment to stay in the city is much more fragile than other conversion residents, as demonstrated by the high proportion (36%) who say they would leave New York City were their rent to double.

The discussion about inducement can be extended to differentiate between legal and illegal residents. In general the illegal residents differ little from the legal residents of lofts, as evident in Exhibit I-13. However, a very small percentage of illegal residents considered more conventional units at the time they moved into their converted unit. Apparently these people, nearly half of whom consider themselves artists, are interested only in the large, flexible, and relatively inexpensive spaces that they can find in lofts, and this interest has been stronger than any qualms they have about living in a unit illegally. Although the illegal residents forsee staying in their unit for a shorter period than legal residents of lofts, their prediction is twice as long as the three years that people living in converted apartments can envision.

And finally, the difference between residents who own their units and those who rent the space, is significant. Only 18 percent of the residents own their units, and they are exclusively in the lofts. Owners are much more satisfied than renters, as shown not only by their scores on the question which asked directly for a satisfaction rating (owners = 4.6, renters = 3.9), but also in the percentage that would choose to live in the unit again (owners = 96%; renters = 78%). And owners foresee staying in their unit 12 years, while renters plan to stay only four years. As was true for people with children, a very high proportion (29%) of owners say they would leave the city were their maintenance fees to double. (This is nearly twice the proportion of renters who say they would leave if their rent doubled). But in the absence of this unhappy circumstance, owners plan to stay in their units twelve years, three times the tenure that renters foresee.

Movements of City Residents to Converted Buildings

As will be described in more detail in Chapter 5 of this study, New York City recently started encouraging the conversion of commercial space to residential use. The vehicle for encouragement is Section J-51 - 2.5 of the Administrative Code of the City of New York, which provides tax benefits to owners of buildings that are converted legally. The previous parts of this chapter, by describing the characteristics of people living in converted structures, have essayed to define the potential beneficiaries of an extended program of tax encouragements. The discussion which follows will consider some information relevant to the workings of the J-51 program thus far.

Rent and Income

In the sample chosen for this study, eleven of the buildings now receive tax abatements. 201 interviews (40 percent of the total) were conducted with residents of these eleven buildings, and from their responses some sense of the effects of the programs can be inferred.

The median rent paid for a unit in a converted building that enjoys a J-51 tax abatement is $375. The rent for a unit in a converted building without the abatement is 8 percent higher, or $405. Income levels are high for all the residents of converted buildings, and they are nearly equivalent for those living in conversions with and without the abatement. The median annual household incomes are $21,602 in units included in the J-51 program, and $21,950 in units that are not included.

Residents of Converted Buildings That Moved From Another Location in New York City

It was noted earlier that 67 percent of the residents of converted buildings had moved there from a location within New York City. It us useful, in trying to assess the attractiveness of converted buildings, to consider the particular locations that residents moved from.

The respondents were not asked for their former address during the original interview. Therefore, a sample of 106 was randomly chosen from the group of conversion residents that had moved from another New York City location, and these residents were asked to give their former address.[8]

Exhibit I-14 shows the results of this analysis, and allows the reader to determine where conversion

EXHIBIT I-14

CONVERTED BUILDING RESIDENTS: PREVIOUS NEW YORK CITY LOCATION

Former NYC Address	*Midtown Central Business District*	*Midtown Loft Area*	*Village*	*Noho*	*Soho*	*Tribeca*
Upper East Side	--	--	17%	--	29%	--
Upper West Side	23%	29%	13%	29%	29%	20%
Midtown CBD	31%	14%	6%	--	--	5%
Midtown Loft Area	8%	14%	7%	14%	--	10%
Village	23%	29%	49%	29%	14%	10%
Noho	8%	--	--	14%	--	10%
Soho	--	--	--	14%	14%	15%
Tribeca	--	--	2%	--	14%	15%
Other Boroughs	7%	14%	6%	--	--	15%
Total	100%	100%	100%	100%	100%	100%

Source: CUPR Interviews of Residents of Converted Buildings, August-September, 1977. This chart is based on a subsample of 106 of the original respondents that had reported moving from within New York City. The interviews of the subsample respondents occurred in October, 1977.

residents are coming from within New York City. The percentages that have boxes drawn around them show the proportion of people living in a converted building in a particular neighborhood that had lived in that neighborhood before their most recent move. For example, 49 percent of the people living in converted buildings in the Village had lived there before. Other items of particular interest are first, that people from the Upper East Side move only into conversions in the Village and Soho; second, that except for the Village, converted buildings in all the neighborhoods are approximately equally populated by residents from the Upper West Side; and third, that Tribeca and the Village are the neighborhoods with the broadest appeal for people moving into converted buildings from other New York City areas.

Movements Into and Out of City-Subsidized Buildings

Within the same subsample described immediately above, it is possible to determine whether the movement of people within New York City to converted buildings has been between buildings subsidized by the city. As mentioned earlier, eleven buildings in the sample have received J-51 tax abatements. Exhibit I-15 shows the type of building that residents of all conversions have moved from, and indicates whether or not the converted building they moved into enjoys benefits of the J-51 program.

EXHIBIT I-15

MOVEMENTS INTO AND OUT OF CITY SUBSIDIZED BUILDINGS

	Current Residence	
Former Residence	*J-51 Tax Beneficiary*	*No J-51 Benefits*
Some type of city subsidy; partial or complete	10%	10%
No subsidy or tax abatement	49%	31%

Source: CUPR Interviews of Residents of Converted Buildings, Subsample (n=106) that had moved from another residence within New York City; October, 1977.

The exhibit shows that some 20 percent of the respondents have come from buildings supported by city funds, and only half of these moved into a conversion with the tax abatement. This means that if the present patterns continue to obtain, and if the city were to greatly expand the number of conversions receiving J-51 abatements, it would be giving subsidies to 20 percent of the population that had received one in the former residence.

SUMMARY

This chapter has presented the facts useful for describing the phenomenon of recycling commercial buildings for residential use. Below are listed the primary findings of this phase of research.

The Recycled Buildings and Dwellings

1. The conversion of buildings from a commercial or industrial use to residential occupancy has been predominantly illegal. The recycled buildings were designed to house non-residential endeavors, and their conversion is illegal either because they are in districts where residential use is prohibited or because they do not meet city standards for inhabitation. Only 10 percent of the conversions are legal.

2. Conversions are of two types. First is conventionally converted space, in which the owner has made a considerable investment in improving space. Once inside the dwelling unit, a tenant would find the small size and appurtenances very similar to an ordinary apartment building. All conventional conversions are legal. The units created in this way are referred to as <u>converted apartments</u>. Second is unconventionally converted space, in which the owner offers a tenant open undifferentiated space and typically does not provide necessities such as kitchens and bathrooms. In general, the owner has made no investment in the conversion and the tenants make all improvements. This type of recycled unit is referred to as a <u>residential loft</u>, and lofts are predominantly illegal.

3. The average converted apartment offers 600 square feet of space, and rents for $393 per month, or $.64 per square foot per month.

4. The average residential loft offers nearly 2100 square feet of space, and rents for $392 per month, or $.19 per square foot per month. The tenants of these large, unimproved spaces spend an average of $7108 on the units for necessary facilities. These figures are for legal and illegal residents.

5. The illegal residents of lofts spend about $390 per month for units that are 2343 square feet in area, and invest $6248 on improvements. The attractions of the large and flexible spaces are sufficient that residents are willing to risk living in and improving places to which they have no claim at law.

The Neighborhoods that Contain Recycled Buildings

1. Converted buildings can be found in two types of neighborhoods. First are conventional neighborhoods, areas that have long been residential, and that offer the typical appurtenant facilities such as schools, parks, and trees. Second are unconventional neighborhoods, areas that have traditionally been commercial, and that offer facilities accessory to trade such as loading docks, but that offer few conveniences for residents.

2. When conversion residents of each type of neighborhood were asked to comment on the area, their responses were remarkably similar. High percentages of residents of both types of areas said the neighborhood was pleasant.

3. Although residents of unconventional neighborhoods receive fewer city services and endure greater inconvenience in obtaining personal services such as groceries, their sense of the importance of city and personal services is no different from what is reported by residents of conventional areas. The converted units available in the unconventional neighborhoods offer amenities that seem to outweigh

the scarcity of city and personal conveniences.

The Residents of Converted Units

1. Converted space is apparently a major attraction to newcomers to New York. More than 30 percent of the occupants moved to their apartments from addresses outside New York City. At the same time, the availability of this housing does not seem to play a critical role in keeping people as city residents. Ninety-two percent of the respondents indicated they would have stayed in New York regardless of whether this special kind of housing had been available or not.

2. People attracted to converted units are young, well paid, and extremely well educated. The median age of conversion residents is 31.8 years (the city-wide median is 44.4 years); the median household income is $21,783 per year (the city-wide median is $9,255); and 74.2 percent of the residents have at least a college degree (10.6 percent of the residents of New York City have an equal achievement).

3. The high educational attainments and the high salaries imply the highly specialized occupations of the conversion residents. Indeed, 56 percent of the converted unit occupants are employed in managerial, professional, and technical positions (for the whole city, 21 percent have these occupations). The conversions house an extremely high proportion of artists, 24 percent as compared to the city-wide proportion of 2 percent. The artists most often occupy illegal lofts, as shown by the 45 percent of these respondents who said they were artists.

4. Large size and attractive, flexible space seem to be the major inducements and satisfaction for people living in converted dwellings. Convenience (proximity to work and shopping) and price were significantly less important as reasons for living in this new kind of housing.

5. Residents of lofts plan to stay in them 8 years,

while people living in the converted apartments foresee staying there only three years.

6. No converted apartments are owned by the residents. People who own their lofts intend to stay there 12 years.

7. The residents as a group are well satisfied with their housing, and would like to stay in New York City. Using a scale from 1 to 5, on which 5 is very satisfied, the residents reported their satisfaction as 4; the large majority would choose to live in the converted unit again. While more than half the residents said they considered living in an apartment building at the time they found the converted space, less than 14 percent reported considering a move to the suburbs. Only 28 percent of the residents of illegally converted lofts considered any other kind of housing. This is probably due in some part to the high proportion of artists who live in the illegal space because they need the extravagant floor area for their artistic pursuits.

The process of recycling commercial and industrial buildings for residential use has succeeded in providing housing attractive to well-educated, relatively affluent people who prefer to live in Manhattan. These are precisely the type of people New York City would like to retain,people who make important contributions to the city's economy both by their being prepared to hold highly-skilled jobs and by their being able to spend money fairly liberally. The latter attribute implies their bolstering the revenues of other workers in the city.

It is important to know if these people are uniquely attracted to the converted units. As a test of this, a study was made of the residents of new apartment buildings, the most prevalent new housing to be found in the city. Chapter 2 describes the results of this study. In Chapter 3 the residents of new apartment buildings are compared to the people living in recycled buildings. In this chapter the unique qualities of each type of tenant will be profiled.

FOOTNOTES

1. Department of City Planning, New York City, Residential Re-Use of Non-Residential Buildings in Manhattan, p. 2.

2. George Sternlieb and James Hughes, Housing and Economic Reality: New York City, 1976. (New Brunswick: Center for Urban Policy Research, 1976), p. 152.

3. Housing and Economic Reality, p. 107, where was given the household income for 1975. This has been inflated at 5 percent per year to compute the 1977 figure used for comparison.

4. Housing and Economic Reality, p. 19.

5. Ibid., p. 83.

6. Ibid., p. 152.

7. U.S. Bureau of the Census, Population and Housing: 1970, PHC(1)-145: New York City, Table p-2.

8. A sample size of 100 is likely to be reliably representative of the group being studied. The Law of Large Numbers provides some assurance of this. Simply stated, this law says that provided the sample size is sufficiently large, the sampling distribution will be approximately normal and is therefore reliable. Statistical literature suggests that whenever the sample size exceeds 100, the information that is gotten from the sample is representative of the population being studied. Further discussion about this can be found in Hubert M. Blalock, Social Statistics, New York: McGraw-Hill Book Company, pp. 138-143.

The building slightly to the left of center in the photograph below receives Section 421 tax benefits. Its very modern design is distinctly different from the older converted building shown on the opposing page.

Frank Gradilone

Frank Gradilone

The entrance to a section 421 building (the photograph with "444 East" shown below revolving doors) appears quite formal compared to the door and doorbells that comprise the entry to a converted building (the photograph with "135" painted on three panels (opposing page).

Kenneth Bleakly, Jr.

Kristina Ford

Chapter 2

NEW APARTMENT BUILDINGS

INTRODUCTION

Chapter 1 described the conversion of commercial and industrial buildings to residential units, a process which recycles old buildings for a new function. Detailed were characteristics of the recycled buildings, the units created, and the tenants attracted to them. This chapter will describe newly constructed multi-family residential buildings and their tenants, and provide a basis for comparison with residents of converted spaces. The newly constructed residential buildings to be discussed are those which receive a partial tax abatement under Section 421 of the Real Property Law of the State of New York,[1] and the buildings will hereafter be referred to as Section 421 housing. The buildings constructed under the inducement of Section 421 were chosen because they account for the largest share of privately sponsored new construction in New York

City,[2] and because the tax abatement which encourages the development of new apartment buildings is similar to the J-51 mechanism which encourages conversions of commercial buildings to residential use. The converted buildings and the Section 421 buildings contain almost all new, privately-financed housing units available in New York City.

The Provisions of Section 421

Section 421 of the Real Property Tax Law was enacted in 1971 to stimulate the production of middle income housing in New York City at a time when there was little new construction. The law offered an abatement on a substantial share of the property taxes owed on a building, and in effect served as a subsidy for part of the costs of operating multiple-family dwellings. The four essential stipulations of Section 421 are for eligible buildings, site requirements, amount of exemption, and reduction in rents. Many of the procedures of Section 421 were modified in 1975, and the following description of the program distinguishes between the original and the amended provisions.

Eligible Buildings

Under the original law, structures had to contain at least 10 units to be eligible. This was changed in 1975 to allow multiple dwellings of six units or more to qualify.[3] As originally enacted, the law emphasized new construction, although rehabilitation was permitted. The 1975 revisions extended the rehabilitation eligibility requirements in recognition of the strength of this part of the housing market. However, since the J-51 Program was modified to allow even greater tax abatements on rehabilitated buildings, the 421 Program has been used almost exclusively for new construction.[4]

Site Requirements

To obtain a tax exemption, new structures must be built on land which is vacant, predominantly vacant, or under-utilized. Rehabilitation can occur where land is under-utilized, occupied by a "functionally obsolete" non-residential building, or has been improved with a nonconforming use.

Amount of Exemption

A building with Section 421 benefits receives a partial tax exemption for 10 years on the value of the improvements made on the property. For the first two years of this period the taxes on the value of the improvements are totally exempt; 80 percent exempt during the second two years; 60 percent exempt during the fifth and sixth years; and are reduced by 20 percent for each subsequent two-year period until there is no exemption in the eleventh year. During the entire ten year exemption period the owner pays taxes on the assessed value of the property prior to the new construction. At no time is there a total exemption from taxes.[5] If the improvements include commercial uses in excess of 12 percent of the aggregate floor area, the exemption allowed the structure is reduced.

Reduction in Rents

The law has changed most substantially with regard to regulation of rent in the Section 421 buildings. Units constructed prior to January 1, 1975, had to offer rents 15 percent below the prevailing rents for newly constructed multiple dwellings. Units constructed after that date do not have a rigid percentage requirement; for these units, rents are determined by an expenditure based formula applied to the detailed operating statement prepared by each owner. A 2.2 percent annual rental increase is permitted to allow for the increasing taxes collected from the owners, and rent control regulations permit another modest increase on top of this property tax pass-through.[6] Owners seeking an abatement after January, 1975, must pay a filing fee equal to 2/10 of 1 percent of the total project cost to cover the added administrative burden imposed by the expenditure analysis procedure for setting rents.

Housing Produced Under the Section 421 Program

Benefits of the Section 421 program have been granted to a great number of housing units created in New York City. Between 1971 and 1973, for example, 88 percent of all private multiple dwelling starts were beneficiaries of Section 421 tax exemptions.[7]

From the inception of the Section 421 program in 1971 until July of 1977, 18,280 units were completed.* There are an additional 11,267 units which have received preliminary certificates and are under some stage of construction.[8] Completed units are located throughout the city and have been constructed in a variety of configurations. As Exhibit II-1 shows, the majority of the completed units (63 percent) are located in Manhattan. The next highest concentration occurs in Queens (24 percent), and the other three boroughs, Brooklyn, the Bronx and Staten Island, share the remaining 13 percent.

The type of project constructed under the Section 421 program varies greatly by borough. In Manhattan the scale of the projects tends to be quite large, with 55 percent of all units located in buildings with 250 units or more, and 7 percent in projects of 100 units or less. Staten Island has no structures with more than 250 units, and 72 percent of all units are in projects of 100 units or less. In fact, many of the projects in Staten Island, Queens and Brooklyn are of the smallest possible size, containing between six and ten units. The Bronx is the only borough other than Manhattan with an appreciable number of large projects, and has 73 percent of all Section 421 units in buildings with at least 500 apartments.

In general, the Section 421 projects vary from the large high-rise apartment buildings near the heart of Manhattan, to smaller six-unit projects in the outlying boroughs. Within Manhattan the Section 421 projects are chiefly concentrated along both the upper and lower East Side, and there is a scattering of projects on the West Side.

A Study of Section 421 Buildings

There have been several studies of the economic workings of Section 421. In an early assessment of the Section 421 program, Jacob Ukeles concluded that costs of foregone taxes were offset by the long-range benefits of the program.[9] George Sternlieb conducted a more rigorous analysis of the program's fiscal impacts

---

*Units completed means buildings which have received at least a Temporary Certificate of Occupancy and are either occupied or ready for occupancy.

EXHIBIT II-1

TOTAL NUMBER OF SECTION 421 HOUSING UNITS COMPLETE (JUNE 6, 1977)

	NUMBER OF UNITS		*SIZE DISTRIBUTION*			
	Number	*Percentage*	*>500 units*	*250-500 units*	*100-250 units*	*<100 units*
Manhattan	11,477	(62.8%)	544 (4.7%)	5,719 (49.8%)	4,386 (38.2%)	828 (7.2%)
Queens	4,309	(23.6)	0 (0.0)	850 (19.7)	1,532 (35.6)	1,927 (44.7)
Staten Island	1,238	(6.8)	0 (0.0)	0 (0.0)	343 (27.7)	895 (72.3)
Brooklyn	452	(2.5)	0 (0.0)	0 (0.0)	243 (53.7)	209 (46.3)
Bronx	804	(4.4)	586 (72.9)	0 (0.0)	0 (0.0)	218 (27.1)
Total	18,280	(100.0)	1,130 (6.2)	6,569 (35.9)	6,504 (35.6)	4,077 (22.3)

Source: N.Y.C. Housing and Development Administration, List of Projects Participating in the Partial Tax Exemption Program, August, 1977.

by evaluating its effects over a twenty-five year period under several assumptions. He concluded that the costs of the Section 421 provisions were probably exceeded by its economic benefits if the multiplier effects of spending induced by the program were taken into account.[10] And more recently, the Citizens Budget Commission estimated that twenty million dollars worth of new construction was generated by the program during 1976, and that this supported between 680 and 850 jobs.[11] For this and other reasons, the Commission concluded that the program has an overall beneficial impact on the city.

What cannot be gotten from these various studies is a sense of the kind of housing units that have been created, or a description of the tenants who live in them. This information will be provided here, as well as a description of the inducement to stay in New York City that Section 421 housing offers its tenants. The material which follows was gotten from interviews conducted in September and October, 1977, with a randomly chosen sample of residents of Section 421 housing. A description of the methodology of the research appears in Appendix B.

The results of the survey of Section 421 residents form the basis of the analysis which follows, and are reported in three parts. The first discusses characteristics of Section 421 buildings, the dwelling units they offer, and the neighborhoods where they can be found. The second part presents profiles of the residents, and the final part tells of the satisfaction of the residents and about the inducements to stay in New York City that these residents feel.

PART I: SECTION 421 BUILDINGS, THE APARTMENTS THEY CONTAIN, AND THE NEIGHBORHOODS WHERE THEY ARE LOCATED

Section 421 Buildings

The newly-constructed buildings that receive Section 421 benefits do not comprise a homogeneous group. There are buildings with over 250 units as well as those with only six apartments; the monthly rents charged range from below $200 to over $600; and the buildings sometimes house commercial enterprises such as grocery stores or travel agencies. These differences separate the Section 421 buildings into two fairly distinct groups according to the borough where the structures are sited.

The first group is to be found in Manhattan, and is characterized by large buildings containing over 250 units (57 percent of the structures), by buildings housing nonresidential uses (58 percent of the structures) and by buildings charging high monthly rents for the apartments (median rent is $506). The second group is comprised of buildings in all other boroughs, and when compared to the first group can be characterized by smaller buildings containing between 100 and 249 units (few structures have more than 250 units), by fewer buildings housing nonresidential uses (36 percent of the structures), and by buildings charging substantially lower monthly rents (median rent is $321). There is no appreciable difference between the two groups when the apartment size is considered, which means that residents of Section 421 buildings in Manhattan pay a premium not for the size of the apartment, but for the location of the building. Exhibit II-2 summarizes the characteristics of Section 421 buildings.

The number of rooms contained in the average Section 421 unit is 3.38 rooms, indicating that these units are slightly smaller than the 3.59 room apartments that are typical of rental housing available in New York City.[12] Three and four room apartments are the most common size available in Section 421 buildings, and this is true for most of the city's rental housing stock. The respondents reported that one-room apartments offer only 443 square feet of living space, and that a four-room apartment is a little more than twice this size, or 1,038 square feet.

The difference between the segment of the rental market served by the Section 421 buildings and the rental housing market in general in New York City is apparent from the wide gap in rents which exists.* The median monthly contract rent for all Section 421 buildings is $465, nearly three times the $171 median contract rent for the city as a whole.[13] None of the Section 421 buildings offer apartments that rent for

---

*The data reported for New York City rental housing stock is for 1975, and is the most recent data available.

EXHIBIT II-2

CHARACTERISTICS OF SECTION 421 BUILDINGS

CATEGORY	Whole Universe Section 421 Buildings	SUBGROUP ANALYSIS Manhattan	Other Boroughs
	n = 505	n = 389	n = 116
Distribution of Units by Building Size			
100 Units or Less	16.2%	7.2%	46.5%
100-249 Units	39.6	35.5	53.4
250+ Units	44.2	57.3	0.0
Non-Residential Uses Present	52.8%	57.7%	36.2%
Number of Rooms in Unit[1]			
1	10.1%		
2	14.7		
3	41.1		
4	22.0	Same as Universe[3]	
5	10.3		
6 or more	1.8		
Median	3.38 rooms		
Median Gross Rent by Number of Rooms[2]			
1	$310	$320	$234
2	420	430	275
3	459	475	320
4	603	622	345
5	690	720	342
6 or more	775	823	399
Median	$465/month	506/month	321/month
Gross Rent Categories			
<$149	0.0%	0.0%	0.0%
150-199	1.3	0.0	5.5
200-249	5.5	0.6	21.8
250-299	12.5	7.8	28.2
300-399	18.0	13.6	32.7
400-499	25.5	30.7	8.2
500-599	17.4	21.9	2.7
600+	19.7	25.5	0.9
Average Unit Size by Number of Rooms			
1	443 sq.ft.		
2	637		
3	782		
4	1028	Same as Universe	
5	1247		
6 or more	*		
Median size	875 sq.ft.		

Notes: 1. Excluding bathrooms
2. Gross rent is the contract rent plus average utility costs.
3. "Same as Universe" means that the responses among the various subgroups were not significantly different from each other, and the response shown in the column titled "Whole Universe of Section 421 Buildings" is the appropriate figure.

Totals may not equal 100% due to rounding.
*insufficient sample size

Source: CUPR Survey of Residents of Section 421 Buildings, October, 1977.

less than $150 per month, but in all of New York City's rental housing stock, 39 percent of the units are available at this price. In the city as a whole, apartments renting for between $200 and $300 per month account for 26 percent of the total rental market, but rentals in this range are available in only 18 percent of the Section 421 units. Rent higher than $300, which is charged in 9 percent of all rental units in New York City is charged in 63 percent of all Section 421 units.

In short, Section 421 buildings are leased at prices that are in the highest ranges of rents found in the city. In part this can be explained by the fact that Section 421 housing is new, that much of it is built near prime residential locations and can command the highest possible value. Also contributing to the high rents is the enormous increase in construction costs during the last several years.

The differences among Section 421 buildings can largely be explained by there being two groups of these structures, the high-rise, high rent Manhattan group, and the more modest scale and moderate cost group sited in the other four boroughs. However, even though there are substantial differences between the rents charged for the units in these two groups, all the Section 421 rentals fall in the upper range of the city's rental housing market, and one fourth of the residents of Section 421 units pay luxury-level prices of at least $600 per month.

Section 421 Units

A good sense of what the units in Section 421 buildings are like can be gotten from the current residents. During the interviews with the tenants, they were asked what had most attracted them to their apartment and what they find most attractive and most detrimental about the unit now that they have lived in it for some time.

The most common reasons residents reported for moving into a Section 421 building are the amenities offered by the particular building or unit, the size of the unit, the convenience to work, and the price. The choice of space as an important reason for moving into a Section 421 apartment may seem incongruous, given the small size of the units that was noted earlier. However, many residents may have moved to a 421 building from an even smaller apartment.

Having lived in the unit a while, the residents find most attractive the design of the apartment and the view. The principal differences between tenants in Manhattan and those in other boroughs are the frequency with which the view and building security are mentioned as attractions. These are approximately three times as important to Manhattan tenants as they are to residents of Section 421 buildings located in the outer boroughs. A point of interest is that although 20 percent of the tenants reported that the space available was the most important reason for choosing the unit, only 9 percent mention this as the most attractive feature after living in the unit.

The negative aspects of living in Section 421 buildings are reported by residents to be mostly related to individual units. The small size of the unit is a major detriment to 23 percent of the households, and price is mentioned by 19 percent. There is not any inherent contradiction between size being reported as a detriment as well as the reason for choosing the apartment. It is possible that the Section 421 apartment is larger than the respondent's previous dwelling, but that he is now unsatisfied and would like a still larger apartment. Other detrimental aspects are the general upkeep and condition of the building, cited by 33 percent of the residents; and the character of the neighborhood, according to 17 percent of the residents.

Dissatisfaction with the size and price of the unit is more common among residents of Section 421 buildings in Manhattan than it is for residents in the outlying boroughs. However, the Manhattan residents complain much less about upkeep of the building and external noise than their counterparts in other boroughs.

Also relevant to this discussion of the Section 421 buildings and units are the tenants' requests for owner-supplied improvements to the buildings. Nearly half the tenants say that no improvements are necessary, one fourth ask for better building maintenance, and the remaining responses are nearly evenly divided among requests for improved security, better appliances, more heat, larger laundry facilities, and other small improvements. This pattern of requests does not vary significantly according to the borough where the Section 421 buildings are located. Exhibit II-3 summarizes the resident's remarks about living in Section 421 buildings.

EXHIBIT II-3

REMARKS BY RESIDENTS OF SECTION 421 ABOUT THEIR HOUSING

CATEGORY	Whole Universe of Section 421 Buildings n = 505	SUBGROUP ANALYSIS	
		Manhattan n = 389	Other Boroughs n = 116
Primary Reason for Moving to Unit			
Amenities, attractiveness of apartment	36.3%	35.3%	40.0%
Space	20.0	21.6	14.7
Nearness to work	15.4	15.9	13.3
Price	14.5	14.9	13.3
Nearness to activities	7.8	5.6	16.0
Price and Space	5.2	5.9	2.7
Most Attractive Feature of Unit			
Design, uniqueness of apt.	20.3%	19.2%	23.5%
View	17.5	20.1	7.8
Proximity to work/school	16.4	15.7	18.6
Amenities of building	14.0	12.7	18.6
Size	9.1	9.1	8.8
Security	6.0	7.2	2.0
Beauty, newness of building	5.4	5.3	5.9
Neighborhood	4.9	5.0	4.9
Price	1.9	1.5	2.0
Appliances	1.3	0.9	2.9
None	3.0	2.6	4.9
Most Detrimental Feature of Unit			
Unit Specific			
Small size	22.6%	25.9%	8.0%
Price	19.3	21.4	10.0
Noise-Internal	7.4	8.1	4.0
Character of the Building			
Poor upkeep/services	23.3	19.1	42.0
Poor building security	5.2	5.5	4.0
Poor building quality	4.8	4.5	6.0
Neighborhood Character			
Noise-external	11.1	9.5	18.0
Undesirable neighborhood	3.3	2.7	6.0
No neighborly contact	3.0	3.2	2.0
Owner Supplied Services Needed or Improvement Necessary			
For the Unit			
Provide heat	4.1		
Better appliances	2.1		
For the Building in General			
Better maintenance	24.9		
Increase security	6.7		
Increase laundry facilities	5.7	Same as Universe[1]	
Better construction	3.6		
Improve semi-public areas	3.1		
Nothing Necessary	48.6		

Note: 1. "Same as Universe" means that the responses among the various subgroups were not significantly different from each other, and the response shown in the column titled "Whole Universe of Section 421 Buildings" is the appropriate figure.

Source: CUPR Survey of Residents of Section 421 Buildings, October, 1977.

The Neighborhoods that Contain Section 421 Buildings

An important factor in the experience of living in any dwelling is its neighborhood. The residents of Section 421 buildings were asked to describe their neighborhood, to rate the importance of the proximity of services, and to specify what city-supplied services would enhance living in the area.

Nearly three quarters of the tenants view their neighborhood as a pleasant place to live. Each respondent was asked to rank the value of being close to a variety of services, using a scale from 1 to 5 on which one means proximity is of no consequence and five means it is of great importance. Close proximity is of greatest importance for food shopping and laundry facilities (4.25 and 4.37 respectively), and the closeness of hardware and houseware stores, luncheonettes, and libraries is considered least essential (2.72, 2.54, 2.67 respectively).

When asked to describe the common characteristics of their neighborhood, three out of four tenants of Section 421 buildings responded positively, citing such factors as cleanliness, safety and quiet (30 percent), and convenience (14 percent). Of those who had negative comments about the neighborhood, the most common complaints are that it is noisy (10 percent), dirty (6 percent), or generally going down hill (5 percent). The most significant difference among responses according to the borough where the Section 421 building is located, is the large percentage of outer borough residents who cited that their neighborhood was going down hill (16 percent). This is nearly seven times the frequency that this response was made by Manhattan residents.

The residents were also asked to name which city-supplied services were most in need of improvement in their neighborhood. Street cleaning and repair, and trash collection are the two most common complaints, and each was mentioned by 14 percent of the tenants. However, 41 percent of the households in Section 421 buildings feel that no improvement in city-supplied services is necessary. This response rate varies by borough, with 39 percent of the Manhattan residents and 51 percent of the outer borough residents saying nothing is necessary. It is difficult to determine if this high percentage indicates a satisfaction with city-supplied services, or if it indicates an acceptance of the fact that services are poorly provided but unlikely to be improved. Data from the Annual Housing Survey for central city households in the Northeast shows levels of satisfaction with city services nearly double what is reported here,[14] and implies that even among the generally affluent residents of many of the better neighborhoods in the city, satisfaction with city services is below regional standards. Exhibit II-4 summarizes the responses made about the neighborhoods by residents of Section 421 buildings.

PART II: THE PEOPLE WHO LIVE IN SECTION 421 BUILDINGS

The discussion thus far has concentrated on Section 421 buildings and units, and the neighborhoods where they are located. This part of the chapter will describe the residents of these new buildings, residents who form a distinct subgroup of the whole New York City renter population.

All Residents of Section 421 Buildings

The residents of Section 421 buildings are young, well-educated, and are employed in high-paying jobs. These characteristics distinguish them from all other renters in New York City prounouncedly. Three-quarters of the respondents are between 20 and 40 years old; the median age is 34.0, much lower than the city median age for all renter households, which was 44.4 years in 1975.[15] The residents of the new buildings have high educational attainments, with 87 percent having completed at least some college or post-secondary education. Only 19 percent of the city's residents have equivalent achievements.

The occupations of the residents of Section 421 buildings are in keeping with their high educational attainments. As seen in Exhibit II-5, 72 percent of the Section 421 residents hold professional, technical, managerial, administrative or proprietary jobs; this is nearly three times the proportion of the city's labor force that holds similar positions. Among lower skilled white collar occupations and blue collar jobs, the residents of the Section 421 buildings are underrepresented when compared to the city-wide proportions.

EXHIBIT II-4

CHARACTERISTICS OF NEIGHBORHOODS CONTAINING SECTION 421 BUILDINGS

CATEGORY	*Whole Universe of Section 421 Buildings n = 505*	*SUBGROUP ANALYSIS*	
		Manhattan n = 389	*Other Boroughs n = 116*
Importance of Proximity to Necessities			
Food shopping	4.25	4.42	3.72
Laundry Facilities	4.37	4.41	4.22
Dry Cleaning	3.73	3.85	3.33
Hardware/Housewares	2.72	2.73	2.67
Bank	3.52	3.48	3.65
Luncheonette	2.54	2.57	2.44
Library	2.67	2.64	2.76
Comments About Their Neighborhood			
Positive			
Safe, Quite/Friendly, Clean	30.4%	31.7%	25.8%
Convenient	13.8	14.9	9.7
Interesting, Varied	11.2	11.7	9.7
Known as Good Neighborhood	10.1	9.8	11.3
Lively, more residential	5.4	7.0	0.0
This street o.k./others bad	2.2	1.4	4.8
Nice in day, frightening at night	0.7	0.4	1.6
Negative			
Very Noisy	10.1	9.8	11.6
Dirty	6.1	5.6	8.1
Area going downhill	5.4	2.3	16.1
Attracts Undesirables	2.9	3.3	1.6
Increasing high rises	1.4	1.9	0.0
City Services in Need of Improvement			
Nothing necessary	41.3%	38.7%	51.2%
Trash collection	14.1	14.9	10.7
Street Cleaning/repair	13.6	14.0	11.9
Public Transportation	8.5	7.9	10.7
Recreation facilities	7.3	7.9	4.8
Police Protection	5.6	5.8	4.8
Parking Facilities	0.7	0.9	0.0
Other	8.5	9.1	6.0

Note: Totals may not equal 100.0% due to rounding.
Source: CUPR Survey of Residents of Section 421 Buildings, October 1977.

EXHIBIT II-5

OCCUPATION BY HEAD OF HOUSEHOLD

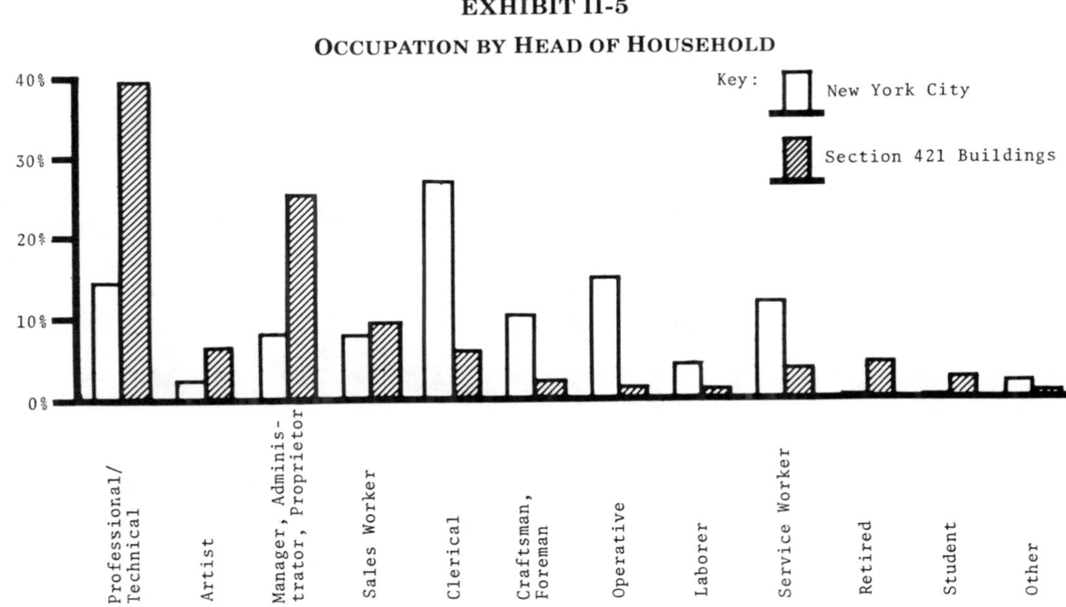

Source: U.S. Bureau of the Census, 1970 Census of Population and Housing: New York SMSA, CUPR Survey of Residents of Section 421 Buildings.

For example, sales and clerical work is the occupation of 15 percent of the Section 421 residents, while 34 percent of the total city labor force is engaged in these kinds of employment.

As would be expected from the occupations of the residents of Section 421 buildings, the median income of these tenants is substantially higher than that earned by all New York City renters. Indeed, the median of $24,268 is about two and half times as high as the city-wide median of $9,255.[16] An analysis of the income subcategories illustrates the wide disparity even more clearly. Among households in Section 421 buildings, 82 percent have incomes of $15,000 or more in 1977; only 21.9 percent of all New York City rental households earn this much. Households with incomes of $5,000 or less represent only 1.4 percent of the Section 421 buildings, but account for 29 percent of all New York City rental households.

Another factor contributing to the high incomes earned by residents of Section 421 buildings is the number of workers per household. As Exhibit II-6 demonstrates, more than half the households that earn at least $35,000 per year contain two or more workers.

EXHIBIT II-6

HOUSEHOLD INCOME BY NUMBER OF FULL-TIME WORKERS

	HOUSEHOLD INCOME				
Number of Workers per Household	*$5,000*	*$5,000-$9,999*	*$10,000 $24,999*	*$25,000-$34,999*	*$35,000+*
0	50.0%	18.8%	8.9$	0.2%	1.1%
1	50.0	75.0	69.2	66.6	42.6
2	0.0	6.3	18.1	31.3	48.9
3	0.0	0.0	3.1	0.0	7.5
4	0.0	0.0	0.6	0.0	0.0
Median Number of workers	0.5	0.9	1.2	1.3	1.6

Source: CUPR Survey of Residents of Section 421 Buildings, October 1977.

Fifty-nine percent of the households in the Section 421 buildings are headed by males, a somewhat smaller proportion than for the whole city (66 percent). And the marital status of members of the households likewise deviates slightly from the city-wide pattern. While almost 50 percent of all adults in the city are married, among residents of Section 421 buildings the figure is 43 percent; divorced households are more common among residents of the new buildings (9 percent) than in New York in general (5 percent).

Several other measures provide useful descriptions of the typical residents of Section 421 buildings. One out of five residents are foreign citizens, the employees of foreign corporations with offices in New York City or members of diplomatic and trade delegations. In general, the residents are racially homogeneous; whites represent 92 percent of the total sample, while among the city's population as a whole blacks number one out of five.

Given the large number of studio and one-bedroom units constructed under the Section 421 program,[17] it is not surprising that the vast majority of households are small. The median household size is 1.6 persons, somewhat smaller than the city-wide median of 2.0 persons per household in rental units in 1975. Only 17 percent of the Section 421 households contain children.

A measure of the affiliation residents of Section 421 buildings feel for the city can be obtained by determining whether they were born in the city or attended school there. Over four in ten of the residents were born in New York City and about the same percentage attended elementary school or college in the city.

The above characteristics yield a profile of the typical Section 421 household. The household head is generally between 20 and 40 years of age, most likely is a male, although female-headed households are more common than for the population of New York City as a whole. The head has completed at least four years of college, is employed in a professional, technical or managerial position and earns a substantial income. There are two adults in the household, both of whom work, and children are rare. The residents are most likely to be white, and a significant number are foreigners.

Characteristics of the Section 421 Residents According to Location

While the typical household residing in a Section 421 building is quite different from the typical renter household in New York City, there are variations which can be attributed to the location of the building receiving Section 421 benefits. The life style associated with Manhattan, its theaters, its shopping and cultural attractions, has a particularly strong attraction to certain segments of the city population, and sets them apart from residents of other boroughs. The scale of construction tends to be very large in Manhattan, and decreases in density and size as the sites are located in the more removed boroughs. The type of person drawn to high-rise living in Manhattan differs in many ways from the residents who live in the lower density, small scale projects found in the other four boroughs.

While residents of all Section 421 buildings have much higher levels of educational achievement than to be found among all New Yorkers, there is a significantly lower percentage of outer borough residents who have completed college (50 percent) than of Manhattan residents (78 percent). And it follows that the occupations are different. Manhattan residents are more often employed in professional and technical occupations (42 percent) than residents in the outer boroughs (34 percent), and clerical employment is significantly greater among the residents of the outer boroughs (13 percent) than among Manhattanites (4 percent).

While all 421 residents have incomes much higher than the typical rental household in the city, there are strong variations between Manhattan and other boroughs. The median income for all Manhattan Section 421 households is $26,300, for the outer boroughs $19,400. In Manhattan, 54 percent of the Section 421 households earn more than $25,000, while in the outer boroughs only 27 percent have incomes above that figure. The outer boroughs have nearly twice the proportion of lower income households ($15,000 or less) that Manhattan has.

There are distinct differences in the sex and the marital status of the Section 421 households residing in Manhattan and in the other boroughs. Over 40 percent of the Manhattan households are female headed, only 30 percent are in the remaining boroughs; and unattached heads of household are more common in Manhattan.

Finally, there is a great degree of variation in the length of time the residents of Section 421 buildings have lived in New York City. One in three have lived in the city for four years or less, while nearly half have lived in the city for more than 10 years (see Exhibit II-7). Residents of Manhattan are less likely to have been long term New Yorkers, with 37 percent having lived in the city at least 10 years, than the residents of other boroughs, where the proportion is nearly two-thirds.

Before moving to their present address, almost two-thirds of the residents of Section 421 buildings had lived elsewhere in New York City. Of the remainder, 19 percent came from a location in the United States beyond the Tri-State region. This is more frequently the case among the Manhattan residents (22 percent), than among outer borough residents (9 percent).

From these differences a bifurcation of residents of Section 421 buildings can be discerned. Those who live in Manhattan have the highest incomes and levels of education, and the most highly skilled occupations. They are more likely to live in female-headed households and households composed of unrelated individuals. There are fewer life-long New Yorkers among the Section 421 households living in Manhattan.

The residents of the outer boroughs have more modest incomes, educational attainments, and occupations. More of the households are headed by males and a majority of the residents are married. They are more likely to have been born and raised in the city than is typical of Manhattan residents. Exhibit II-8 summarizes the characteristics of all residents of Section 421 buildings, and of the residents when they are considered as two groups, those who live in Manhattan and those who live in the boroughs of the Bronx, Queens, Brooklyn, and Staten Island.

PART III: SATISFACTION AND INDUCEMENT

The Section 421 program was designed to stimulate the construction of new middle-income housing in New

EXHIBIT II-7

PREVIOUS RESIDENCE INFORMATION

CATEGORY	*Whole Universe of Section 421 Buildings*	*SUBGROUP ANALYSIS*	
		Manhattan	*Other Boroughs*
	n = 505	*n = 389*	*n = 116*
Length of Residence in NYC			
4 years or less	33.1%	38.8%	18.1%
5-9 years	22.2	23.9	16.4
10 years or more	43.8	37.3	65.5
Location of Previous Residence			
New York City - Total	60.6%	55.0%	79.9%
Manhattan	(33.3)	(40.1)	(10.3)
Bronx	(13.1)	(5.1)	(39.7)
Brooklyn	(3.4)	(3.1)	(4.3)
Queens	(8.1)	(6.7)	(12.9)
Staten Island	(2.8)	(0.0)	(12.1)
New York Metropolitan Region[1]			
Tri-State Region[2]	7.7	8.7	4.3
Other U.S.	6.1	6.4	5.2
Foreign	18.6	21.6	8.7
	6.3	7.9	1.7

Notes: [1]The New York Metropolitan Region is the 22 county region as defined by the Port Authority and Regional Plan Association, except for the five boroughs of N.Y.C.

[2]The Tri-State Region is New York, New Jersey, and Connecticut, except for New York City and the Metropolitan Region.

Source: CUPR Survey of Residents of Section 421 Buildings, October 1977.

EXHIBIT II-8

PERSONAL CHARACTERISTICS OF THE RESIDENTS OF 421 BUILDINGS

CATEGORY	New York City[1]	Whole Universe of Residents of Section 421 Buildings n = 505	SUBGROUP ANALYSIS Manhattan n = 389	Other Boroughs n = 116
Age of Household Head				
Less than 20 years	N.A.	0.0%	0.0%	0.0%
20-29		35.0	34.7	36.1
30-39		40.5	42.0	35.2
40-49		9.9	9.2	12.0
50-59		7.1	7.0	7.4
60 and over		7.5	7.0	9.3
Sex of Household Head	(1975)			
Male	66.3%	59.5%	56.5%	69.7%
Female	33.7	40.5	43.5	30.3
Marital Status of Household Head	(1970)			
Single	34.9	44.1%	48.5%	29.1%
Married	49.5	43.5	39.0	58.2
(Separated)	(5.6)	(3.8)	(4.6)	(0.9)
Divorced	5.0	8.6	8.9	7.3
Widowed	10.6	4.0	3.5	5.5
Schooling Completed by Household Head	(1970)			
0-7 Grades	19.6%	0.0%	0.0%	0.0%
8-11 Grades	33.5	1.3	0.5	3.7
Completed High School	28.3	11.4	7.6	24.3
Some College or Post-Secondary	8.1	16.0	14.1	22.4
4 or More Years of College	10.6	71.3	77.7	49.5
Occupation	(1970)			
Professional/ Technical[2]	13.6%	39.9%	41.7%	33.9%
Artist	2.1	6.8	8.8	0.0
Manager, Administrator, Proprietor	7.8	25.9	26.0	25.7
Sales Worker	7.3	9.1	9.9	6.4
Clerical	27.1	6.4	4.4	12.8
Craftsman, Foreman	10.2	1.9	1.1	4.6
Operative	15.0	1.1	0.3	3.7
Laborer	3.3	0.6	0.3	1.8
Service Worker	12.3	2.8	2.2	4.6

(continued)

EXHIBIT II-8 *(continued)*

PERSONAL CHARACTERISTICS OF THE RESIDENTS OF 421 BUILDINGS

CATEGORY	New York City[1]	Whole Universe of Residents of Section 421 Buildings n = 505	SUBGROUP ANALYSIS Manhattan n = 389	Other Boroughs n = 116
Occupation (continued)				
Retired	-	3.4	2.5	6.4
Student	-	1.9	2.5	0.0
Other	1.3	0.2	0.3	0.0
Citizenship of Household Head				
United States	N.A.	79.2%	81.0%	72.4%
Foreign		20.8	19.0	27.6
Race of Household Head	(1975)			
White[3]	70.9%	91.6%	95.1%	79.8%
Black	23.8	4.8	3.0	11.0
Other	5.3	3.6	1.9	9.2
Household Income[4]	(1975)			
Less than $5,000	29.0%	1.4%	1.8%	0.0%
$ 5,000 - $ 9,999	29.4	3.9	2.7	7.6
$10,000 - $14,999	19.7	12.7	9.7	21.9
$15,000 - $19,999 }		15.9	13.7	22.9
$20,000 - $24,999 }		18.9	18.2	21.0
$25,000 - $29,999 }	21.9	14.1	14.6	12.4
$30,000 - $34,999 }		10.6	10.9	9.5
$35,000 - $49,999 }		12.0	14.9	2.9
$50,000+ }		10.6	13.4	1.9
Median	$8,395	$24,268	$26,302	$19,479
Persons in Household	(1975)			
1	33.7%	42.8%	44.9%	35.8%
2	30.5	41.1	42.5	36.7
3	15.2	11.8	10.1	17.4
4 or more	20.6	4.2	2.4	9.1
Median	2.0 people	1.6 people	1.6 people	1.7 people
Children in the Household				
0	N.A.	82.9%	87.0%	69.1%
1		12.2	10.4	18.1
2		2.4	0.9	7.4
3		1.5	1.3	2.1
4 or more		1.0	0.3	3.2

(continued)

EXHIBIT II-8 *(continued)*

PERSONAL CHARACTERISTICS OF THE RESIDENTS OF 421 BUILDINGS

CATEGORY	*New York City*[1]	*Whole Universe of Residents of Section 421 Buildings n = 505*	*SUBGROUP ANALYSIS Manhattan n = 389*	*Other Boroughs n = 116*
New York City Affiliation				
Born in New York City	N.A.	43.4%	40.8%	51.8%
Went to Elementary or High School in NYC		39.9	33.5	61.5
Went to College in NYC		47.6	47.8	46.7

Notes: [1]Where indicated, New York City figures are either for the city population as a whole in 1970 or renter households in 1975.

[2]The category "artist" which is normally included in the totals for professional/technical workers has been disaggregated for comparative purposes.

[3]Hispanics are included as whites.

[4]These income figures are from the U.S. Bureau of the Census,1975 New York City Housing and Vacancy Survey as reported in Sternlieb and Hughes, Housing and Economic Reality. For each of these categories the percentages are of those households which reported incomes. Of the 421 sample, 14 percent; and of the total rental population in 1975, 29 percent; did not report their incomes.

Numbers may not total 100.0 percent due to rounding.

Source: Center for Urban Policy Research, Rutgers University, Survey of Section 421 Residents, October 1977. U.S. Bureau of the Census, Detail Population Characteristics, Part 34, New York. George Sternlieb and James Hughes, Housing and Economic Reality (New Brunswick, N.J., 1976).

York City by offering tax benefits to owners. Completed units numbered 18,280 by July of 1977, and preliminary certificates for another 11,267 units have been issued. The program could be called successful simply because so many housing units have been created since its inception. But success can also be gauged by expressions of satisfaction made by residents, and by the inducement to stay in New York City that the Section 421 buildings provide their tenants.

Satisfaction of Residents of Section 421 Buildings

The sense gotten from the interviews with residents of Section 421 buildings is one of satisfaction with their housing. Using a scale from one to five, on which five is very satisfied and one is very unsatisfied, the mean for all these residents is 3.8. The Manhattan tenants are somewhat more satisfied (3.9), and the outer borough residents are slightly less pleased (3.6). When asked whether they would again choose to live in their Section 421 unit, nearly three quarters of the residents responded that they would. This corroborates the fairly high level of satisfaction that is reported.

Those who would not choose the Section 421 unit again were asked the type of housing most appealing to them. Suburban housing units would be preferred by four in ten of the dissatisfied residents, another 10 percent would choose a loft structure, 15 percent would rather live in a brownstone or townhouse, and 21 percent wanted any type of housing that is larger. Residents in Manhattan are more interested in obtaining a larger unit and less interested in suburban housing than other residents; these others predominantly prefer suburban housing.

The residents of Section 421 buildings intend to stay in their units for an average of 2.4 years. Those who said that they intended to stay less than three years, 81 percent of the respondents, were asked where they planned to go next. Slightly more than one in two plan to find accommodations elsewhere in New York City. Over 20 percent anticipate moving away from the Tri-State region altogether. The residents from the outer boroughs show a greater desire to move into other locations in the region and less of an insistence on remaining in the city.

When the respondents were queried about their reasons for wanting to move, they did not evidence a clear pattern of dissatisfaction. The most frequently cited reasons are a desire for more space (23 percent), the hope of a cheaper unit (21 percent), or an anticipated change in employment (16 percent). Residents of the outer boroughs rarely cited change of employment as their reason for moving (2 percent), and more often said they wanted to own their residence.

Since most of the residents of Section 421 buildings intend to move within three years, it is interesting to find out how attracted they are to living in converted buildings, a relatively new housing option in New York City. Eighty-two percent of the residents had heard of people living in lofts in converted structures. Of these, about half said they would consider moving into such a unit, and cited their attractive qualities to be increased space, light and air (26 percent), and greater interior flexibility because of the unconventional layout of the units (16 percent). The primary reasons for not considering this new type of housing are a general distaste for them and a dislike for the neighborhoods in which converted buildings are located (see Exhibit II-9). It seems there is a significant subgroup of residents of newly constructed buildings who are interested in, or at least initially receptive to, the idea of loft living.

Exhibit II-10 summarizes the various measures of satisfaction discussed. Although the typical residents of Section 421 buildings do not intend to stay longer than two and a half years, they do seem fairly well satisfied with their apartments. Disgruntled residents look most favorably upon suburban housing or larger apartments as an alternative, and are less attracted to brownstones and lofts. The pull of suburbia is weaker in Manhattan and considerably stronger among the residents in the outlying boroughs.

Only about one half of the residents foresee themselves remaining in the city. The Manhattan residents who plan to move cite the need for more space, employment changes, and changes in family status as the primary reasons for moving. Outer borough residents are drawn out of the city by the desire to own a house.

Lofts, which have recently captured a great deal of popular attention, are very attractive to those households seeking more light and air, a better size-to-price ratio, or an unconventional dwelling. Those who remain cool to loft living dislike the housing type and the neighborhoods where they are located.

EXHIBIT II-9

INTEREST IN CONVERTED BUILDINGS

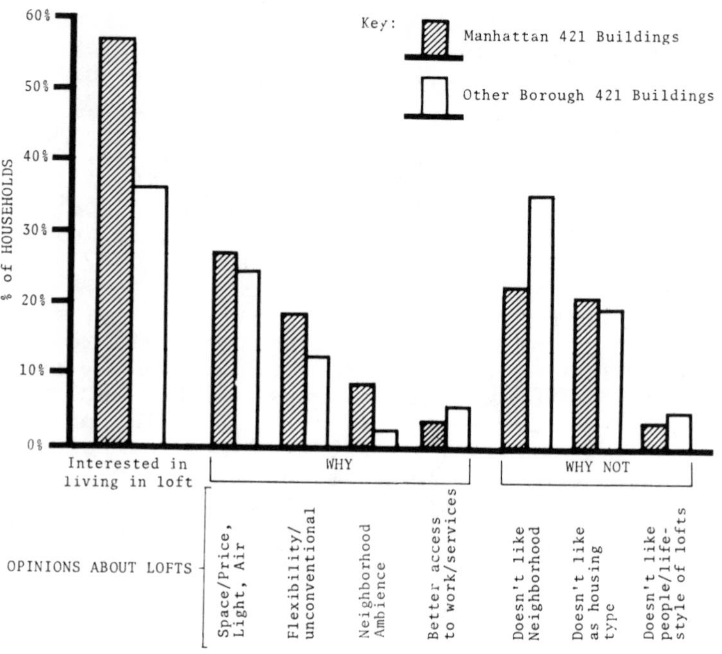

Source: CUPR Survey of Residents of Section 421 Buildings

EXHIBIT II-10

SATISFACTION OF RESIDENTS OF SECTION 421 BUILDINGS

CATEGORY	Whole Universe of Section 421 Buildings n = 505	SUBGROUP ANALYSIS	
		Manhattan n = 389	Other Boroughs n = 116
Level of Satisfaction	3.8	3.9	3.6
Would Not Choose to Live in A Similar Unit Again	26.6%	25.1%	31.6%
Type of Housing Preferred			
Suburban Housing	40.7%	31.8%	64.0%
Larger Unit	20.9	27.3	4.0
Brownstone/Townhouse	15.3	18.2	8.0
Renovated Building	9.8	12.1	4.0
A more luxurious building	6.6	4.5	12.0
A cooperative or condominium	5.4	4.5	8.0
Building with more security	1.1	1.5	0.0
Length of Time Tenant Intends to Stay in Unit	2.39 years	Same as Universe[1]	
If Staying in Unit Less Than Three Years, Where They Plan to Move (n = 407)			
Elsewhere in New York City	52.3%	53.8%	46.3%
New York Metropolitan Area	13.6	11.4	22.2
Tri-State Region	6.8	6.2	9.3
Other	27.8	28.6	22.2
If Staying in Unit Less Than Three Years, Reason for Moving			
Wants more space	22.8%	23.2%	21.3%
Cost is too great	21.1	20.4	23.4
Change in employment	15.8	19.3	2.1
Wants to own residence	10.5	7.7	21.3
Less distance from work	9.2	9.9	6.4
Change in family status	9.2	9.3	8.5
Wants to leave NYC	7.5	7.1	8.5
Better building services	2.2	1.1	6.4
To be closer to recreation or culture	1.8	1.7	2.1
Interested in Loft Housing	53.6%	57.8%	37.0%
Reasons Why/Why Not			
Why			
Space/price, light, air	26.2%		
Interior flexibility/unconventional layout	15.7		
Neighborhood ambiance	6.4		
Better access to work/services	3.4	Same as Universe	
Why Not			
Doesn't like neighborhood	24.3		
Doesn't like the housing type	20.6		
Doesn't like people or life style of lofts	3.4		

Note: [1]"Same as Universe" means that the responses among the various subgroups were not significantly different from each other and the response shown in the column titled "Whole Universe of Section 421 Buildings) is the appropriate figure.

Totals may not equal 100.0% due to rounding.

Source: CUPR Survey of residents of Section 421 Buildings, October 1977.

Inducement to Stay in New York City

One of the chief concerns of this research effort is to assess how effective tax abatement strategies are in keeping residents in the city through the provision of improved housing opportunities. To arrive at some measure of this, a series of questions was asked concerning the attractiveness of the suburbs as a place of residence, and the level of commitment of the residents to their present housing type. These questions offer an indication of how likely the residents of Section 421 buildings are to stay in New York City.

Twenty percent of the respondents said that at the time they decided to move into an apartment in a Section 421 building, they had considered moving to the suburbs. Residents of Manhattan showed a slightly lower preference for suburbia (16 percent), and residents of the outer boroughs a much stronger inclination (35 percent).

The residents of these new units were asked whether they would have left the city if a similar unit had not been available, and 14 percent said that they would have. This small percentage, when considered in combination with the great variety of housing types which appeal to the residents for their next home, indicates that the amenities of Section 421 apartments are not perceived to be the essential element keeping a tenant in the city.

As another measure of the alternative housing preferences of the residents of Section 421 apartments, each respondent was asked what he would do if his rent or maintenance fee doubled. Half of these tenants responded that they would remain in New York City and make some type of adjustment. Twenty-two percent said they would seek housing at a cheaper price, not necessarily similar to their Section 421 unit. Sixteen percent would seek another apartment unit, and only 4 percent of the residents said they would look for a brownstone or a converted loft. Residents of the outer boroughs showed a weaker preference for remaining in the city (30 percent). One quarter of the residents of Section 421 units said they would seek housing outside the city, most frequently citing suburban single family housing as their first choice. Finally, 25 percent of the residents simply stated that they would move should their housing costs double, but were not specific about location and housing type they would select (see Exhibit II-11).

EXHIBIT II-11

INDUCEMENT TO STAY IN NEW YORK CITY

CATEGORY	*Whole Universe of Residents of Section 421 Buildings n = 505*	*SUBGROUP ANALYSIS Manhattan n = 389*	*Other Boroughs n = 116*
When Respondent Decided to Move Into Current Unit, Considered Moving to Suburbs	20.6%	16.3%	35.1%
Resident would have left City if Similar Unit Had Not Been Available	13.7%	12.8%	16.8%
If Rent or Maintenance Fee Doubled:			
Would Stay in NYC:	50.4%	53.8%	38.8%
Find a cheaper place	21.7	23.5	15.5
Move to another apartment	15.6	17.4	9.7
Pay the increase	6.0	5.5	7.8
Move to a brownstone/ townhouse	2.5	2.3	2.9
Move to a loft	1.8	2.0	1.0
Move to another borough	1.5	1.4	1.9
Get more people to share rent	1.3	1.7	0.0
Would Leave NYC:	25.1%	22.9%	32.1%
Move to suburbs/single family home	9.6	8.1	14.6
Location unspecified	6.7	6.7	6.8
Move outside NY region	5.5	4.9	6.8
Move to suburbs/apartment	3.3	3.2	3.9
Move to an Unspecified Location	24.5%	23.2%	29.1%

Note: Totals may not equal 100.0% due to rounding.

Source: CUPR Survey of 421 Residents, October 1977.

The importance of newly constructed apartments in holding families in the city is difficult to judge. When confronted with the possibility of greatly escalated housing costs, the largest percentage of residents stated they would remain in the city and look for cheaper housing. When asked earlier about the most favorable feature of their apartments, most comments were about the unique design quality of the units, the view, and the convenience to work and recreation. From these pieces of information, as well as the relatively weak attraction of the suburbs, it could be inferred that the Section 421 buildings provide an attractive package of housing services, but that their location is their most important quality to those of middle to upper income. This seems a particularly likely inference for residents of Manhattan where the Section 421 program expands the quantity of housing available in desirable neighborhoods where apartments are in great demand. Most of this housing is provided at a very high rental, with 26 percent of the Manhattan tenants paying $600 or more per month. By increasing the housing available in New York City's better neighborhoods, the Section 421 program has built upon the quality of life found in these areas and added to the city's supply of attractive middle and upper income housing.

SUMMARY

Section 421 buildings are newly-built, multi-family residential structures that receive tax benefits under the provisions of Section 421 of the Real Property Law of the State of New York. They have been chosen for study because they comprise the largest share of privately-sponsored new construction in New York City and because the provisions of the Section 421 tax benefits program are similar to the J-51 mechanism which encourages conversions of commercial buildings to residential use.

This chapter has provided a description of these newly built apartment houses, the people who live in them, and the importance of the apartments in keeping tenants in New York City. The most important findings are listed below.

The Section 421 Buildings and Apartments

1. From the inception of the Section 421 Program in 1971 until July, 1977, 18,280 units were

completed. An additional 11,267 units have received preliminary certification to be constructed.

2. The type of building receiving Section 421 benefits varies greatly by borough. In Manhattan, 55 percent of all units are in buildings that contain at least 250 apartments; in all the other boroughs there is a substantial number of six-family structures and only 21 percent of the units are in large buildings.

3. The median monthly rent for a Section 421 apartment in Manhattan is $506; in the other boroughs it is $321. These medians and the distribution of rents charged mean that the cost of Section 421 apartments is in the highest ranges of rents found in New York City.

4. The tenants of Section 421 units choose to live in them chiefly because of their amenities, their size, their convenience, or their price. Apartments which have a view and buildings with security systems are nearly three times as important to Manhattan residents as to residents of the other four boroughs.

5. Nearly three quarters of the tenants of Section 421 apartments think that their neighborhoods are pleasant. Although four tenths of the residents do not think any additional city services are necessary to improve their neighborhoods, approximately 30 percent think that street cleaning and repair, and garbage collection should be improved.

The Residents of Section 421 Buildings

1. These newly constructed buildings attract about 45 percent of their residents from places other than New York City. However, the units do not seem to provide the most important inducement to stay in the city, since 86 percent of the residents would have stayed in New York City if a similar unit had not been available.

2. People attracted to Section 421 units are young, well-paid, and highly educated. While in the city as a whole 21 percent of the workers are

employed in professional, technical, managerial, administrative, or proprietary jobs, 72 percent of the Section 421 residents pursue these occupations. The median age is 33.6 years, much lower than the citywide median of 44.4 years. Finally, the median household income is $24,268, about two and a half times the city-wide median of $9,255.

3. There are usually two adults in the household, and only 17 percent of the households have children. The household is headed by a woman in 41 percent of the units.

4. Residents of Section 421 buildings in Manhattan are somewhat younger, are better educated, are more often employed in highly-skilled jobs, and earn more money than residents of these buildings sited in the other boroughs.

5. As a group, the residents are fairly well satisfied. Using a scale from one to five, where five is very satisfied, the mean level of satisfaction is 3.8. Residents in Manhattan are somewhat more satisfied (3.9) than outer borough tenants (3.6). An additional indication of satisfaction is that nearly three-quarters of the tenants would choose again to live in their unit.

6. Residents of Section 421 apartments intend to stay in them an average of 2.4 years. Eighty-one percent plan to stay less than 3 years, and of these a little more than half anticipate moving to another location in New York City, while 20 percent intend to move away from the New York City Metropolitan Region entirely.

7. When confronted with the possibility of greatly escalted housing costs, the largest portion of residents said they would remain in the city and look for cheaper housing. From this and other measures of satisfaction and inducement, it could be inferred that Section 421 buildings provide an attractive housing option, but that their location is their most important attribute, particularly for the structures in Manhattan.

FOOTNOTES

1. §421 of the Real Property Tax Law, State of New York, amended by Chapter 703 of the Laws of 1976.

2. Dana Fankuchen, A Review of Real Estate Tax Incentive Programs in New York City, March 1977 (New York: Citizens Budget Commission, Inc., 1977), p. iv.

3. Housing and Development Administration, Rules and Regulations Governing 421 Partial Tax Exemption, 10/20/1976, Section 2.

4. Interview with Mr. Paul Schultz, Partial Tax Abatement Administrator, New York City Housing and Development Agency, 12/77.

5. Rules and Regulations Governing 421 Partial Tax Exemption, Section 8.

6. Rates of increase above that allowed for the increase in tax payments are determined by the New York City Rent Guidelines Board.

7. Fankuchen, A Review of Real Estate Tax Incentive Programs, p. 15.

8. Interview with Mr. Leo Loher, Housing and Development Administration, 11/77.

9. Jacob Ukeles, et al., An Assessment of the Section 421 Limited Tax Exemption Program: Interim Report (New York City: Center for New York City Affairs, New School for Social Research, 1975), p. 4.

10. George Sternlieb, Elizabeth Roistacher, and James Hughes, Tax Subsidies and Housing Investment (New Brunswick: Center for Urban Policy Research, 1976) p.6.

11. Fankuchen, A Review of Real Estate Tax Incentive Programs, pp. 16-17.

12. George Sternlieb and James Hughes, Housing and Economic Reality: New York City, 1976 (New Brunswick, N.J.: Center for Urban Policy Research, 1976), p.60.

13. Ibid., p. 111.

14. U.S. Bureau of the Census, Annual Housing Survey: 1975 United States and Region Series H-150-75B, Indicators of Housing and Neighborhood Quality (Washington, D.C., Government Printing Office, 1977).

15. Sternlieb and Hughes, Housing and Economic Reality, p. 19.

16. Ibid. This has been inflated at 5 percent per year to compute the 1977 figure used for comparison.

17. Ukeles, et al., An Assessment of the Section 421 Limited Tax Exemption Program, p. 14.

Kristina Ford

Frank Gradilone

conventional neighborhood is pictured above, showing many people on the sidewalks side stores that cater to a residential area. An unconventional neighborhood appears the opposing page, where the facilities are designed to commercial and industrial use.

Chapter 3

SALVAGED BUILDINGS AND NEW BUILDINGS: A COMPARISON

INTRODUCTION

Residential buildings newly constructed under the benefits of the Section 421 program and buildings converted to housing from former commercial or industrial uses are by far the largest sources of privately created new dwelling units in New York City. By encouraging the continued new construction and conversion, the city hopes to attract or retain residents who contribute to the city economy through their spending and their occupational skills. The preceding chapters of this volume have shown that the current residents of Section 421 buildings and of converted buildings are generally highly skilled and highly paid. This chapter will contrast the tenants of new apartment buildings (the Section 421 structures) with residents of converted buildings. This comparison is necessary if the city intends to encourage with tax benefits both new construction (Section 421 tax benefits) and conversion (J-51 tax benefits), because it will make clear who the recipients are of the benefits of each program.

Chapter 2 described the Section 421 buildings, showing that there is a significant difference between buildings in Manhattan and buildings in the other four boroughs. In addition, all the converted buildings under study are in Manhattan. Therefore, this chapter will compare converted buildings with Section 421 buildings in Manhattan.

Buildings that have been converted from commercial or industrial uses into units for residential occupancy can be separated into two types of structures. First are those that have been refashioned into conventional dwelling units, units that are little different from those available in apartment buildings with regard to space or the fixtures provided such as bathrooms and kitchens. The second type of converted building offers very large areas of living space, and often does not include any fixtures. Chapter 1 distinguished between these two types of converted units, referring to the first type as converted apartments and to the second type as lofts. This distinction will be continued in this chapter.

CHARACTERISTICS OF THE BUILDINGS AND UNITS

The external differences between Section 421 buildings and converted buildings are immediately apparent. All Section 421 buildings are new, and most of them contain more than 250 apartments. The converted buildings are older; their architecture represents the fashion of their day and heralds their former commercial or industrial use. Converted apartments are usually found in a building that contains 130 units; lofts are typically in buildings with only 12 units.

The units within the buildings can be usefully compared. Section 421 apartments and converted apartments are similar to each other, while the lofts are unique. Average unit size in the Section 421 buildings in Manhattan is 875 square feet, relatively similar to the average of 610 square feet reported by residents of converted apartments, and significantly smaller than the 2,100 square feet reported by residents of lofts. These figures deserve some qualification. The residents were asked the dimensions of their units, and the responses were not verified by measuring the area. The figure given for the lofts is probably fairly accurate, since these units are usually advertised principally in terms of their size. On the other hand, people living in the Section 421 apartments and the converted apartments, particularly those who think their unit small, may underestimate the area of the dwelling. However, even if the disparity is not as great as the residents report, the size of the lofts is probably substantially larger than the apartments of either type.

The median monthly rent paid for a Section 421 apartment is $506, higher than the $392 paid for either type of unit in a converted building. Lofts are the cheapest per square foot of space, costing about one-third that of converted apartments or Section 421 apartments. Apartments in the Section 421 buildings are more expensive than units in the converted buildings in large part because of the location. Most of the 421 buildings are sited in desirable Manhattan neighborhoods, locations typically more expensive than where conversions have occurred. The average rent paid in New York City was $171 in 1975. Even allowing for inflation, it should be remarked that the difference between the rent paid for the Section 421 apartments and for the converted units and lofts is much less than the difference between what the average New York City renter pays and what the resident of a loft, a converted apartment, or a Section 421 apartment pays.

Exhibit III-1 summarizes the most important attributes of the three kinds of dwelling units being discussed. From this exhibit and from the discussions in Chapters 1 and 2, it is clear that there are several housing options represented by all the survey work. At one extreme are Section 421 buildings, which are typically high rise, modern buildings on the Upper East Side, a desirable and traditionally residential area. There are few surprises to be found in the apartments here - they are small, expensive, and located in neighborhoods with ample residential amenities such as parks. At the other extreme are small buildings in industrial neighborhoods with very large, unimproved lofts available for the enterprising tenant willing to install bathrooms or a kitchen, and sand the floors.

EXHIBIT III-1

CHARACTERISTICS OF BUILDINGS

CATEGORY	Manhattan Section 421 Buildings	CONVERTED BUILDINGS Converted Apartments	Residential Lofts
Average Number of Units	210	131	12
Number of Rooms in Unit[1]			
1	10.1%	26.6%	28.1%
2	14.7	25.9	17.0
3	41.1	30.9	19.2
4	22.0	11.5	13.4
5	10.3	4.0	7.6
6 or more	1.8	1.1	14.7
Median	3.4 rooms	2.4 rooms	3.1 rooms
Average Area of Unit	875 sq.ft.	610 sq.ft.	2090 sq.ft.
Rent Paid Per Month			
Per unit	$506	$393	$392
Per Square Foot	$.58	$.64	$.19

Notes: 1. Excluding bathrooms.

Source: CUPR Survey of Residents of Section 421 Buildings, October 1977; CUPR Survey of Residents of Converted Buildings, August-September 1977.

There are surprises here - the space can be used more creatively and designed more uniquely than can a small apartment that has all cooking and plumbing needs supplied. There are also surprises in the industrial neighborhoods, such as the quiet, even rural, atmosphere that comes over these districts at night after the industrial enterprises close. Between the two extremes are buildings with converted apartments (some surprises in aesthetic qualities such as vaulted windows) in industrial areas (some surprises in neighborhood characteristics), or buildings that offer lofts (surprising amount of living space that can be individually designed) in residential neighborhoods with ample amenities.

The surveys of residents of converted buildings and of Section 421 buildings asked for the primary reason that the particular unit was chosen by the tenant, what the tenant found to be most attractive and most detrimental after living in the unit, and what owner-supplied services would improve the experience of living in the unit. These responses were discussed in Chapters 1 and 2, and are shown in Exhibit III-2 for comparison with each other. This exhibit includes the five most frequently made responses to the questions, and represents the large portion of all remarks made. The decision to present only the most frequent responses is for ease of comparison of the most salient qualities. The full range of responses appears in the preceding two chapters.

If the space contained in a unit is considered an amenity, then loft residents and Section 421 residents chose their unit principally because of its amenities or attractiveness. Location seems a more important factor for the converted apartment dwellers. After living in the unit for a while, a different pattern of responses appears. Adding the mention of a view to other qualities of design or uniqueness, it is seen that the unit's qualities are mentioned least often by Section 421 residents, most often by loft residents, and converted apartment residents fall in between the other two. The reverse of this pattern appears when residents are asked to name the most detrimental quality of their unit. Section 421 residents most often mention small size and price, loft residents mention these least often, and converted apartment tenants again fall in between. No single pattern of responses can be found among these residents. However, there is a

EXHIBIT III-2

REMARKS ABOUT THE UNITS MADE BY RESIDENTS

CATEGORY	*Manhattan Section 421 Units n = 389*	*CONVERTED BUILDINGS*	
		Converted Apartments n = 278	*Residential Lofts n = 224*
Primary Reason for Moving to Unit			
Amenities, attractiveness of unit[1]	35.3%	16.5%	24.3%
Space	21.6	19.1	37.6
Nearness to work	15.9	16.9	4.6
Price	14.9	10.6	16.2
Nearness to activities	5.6	14.8	4.1
Most Attractive Feature of Unit			
View	20.1%	8.7%	14.1%
Design, uniqueness of apartment	19.2	41.1	45.5
Proximity to work or school	15.7	5.8	0.9
Amenities of building[2]	12.7	14.2	3.7
Size	9.1	12.4	27.3
Most Detrimental Feature of Unit			
Specific to Unit or Building			
Small size	25.9%	14.5%	7.1%
Price	21.9	6.3	4.7
Poor upkeep or services in building	19.1	16.0	18.9
Noise-Internal	8.1	9.7	2.4

(continued)

EXHIBIT III-2 *(continued)*

REMARKS ABOUT THE UNITS MADE BY RESIDENTS

CATEGORY	*Manhattan Section 421 Units* *n = 389*	*CONVERTED BUILDINGS* *Converted Apartments* *n = 278*	*Residential Lofts* *n = 224*
Specific to Neighborhood			
Noise-External	9.5%	5.9%	15.6%
Owner-Supplied Services to Improve Living in the Unit			
Nothing Necessary	48.6%	38.6%	47.5%
Better Maintenance	24.9	27.2	23.0
Increase Security	6.7	9.3	3.8
Increase Laundry Facilities	5.7	1.6	3.8
Increase or Provide Heat	4.1	2.4	2.7

Notes: 1. This includes both attractiveness or amenities of the unit and of the building.
2. This includes amenities such as a spa and the beauty or unique quality of the building.

Source: CUPR Survey of Residents of Section 421 Buildings, October 1977; CUPR Survey of Residents of Converted Buildings, August-September, 1977.

great similarity in the respondents' sense of what owner-supplied services would improve the experience of living in each of the three types of units. The largest proportion thinks that nothing is necessary; and approximately a quarter of the residents of each type of building askes for better maintenance.

The largest portion of these residents appears to be able to choose a place to live in New York City based on some physical attribute of a particular unit. Although artists often say that they can only afford to rent or own workspace and living space when it is offered in combination as in the lofts, most of the other residents do not seem to be particularly strongly influenced by the price of a unit. They appear to be able to afford to live wherever the amenities and the location suit them.

As Exhibit III-3 demonstrates, there are not many differences in the way that residents perceive their neighborhoods. In this exhibit a slightly different comparison is being made than elsewhere in this chapter. As Chapter 1 described, converted buildings are located either in neighborhoods traditionally residential or in areas traditionally devoted to trade. The former are called conventional neighborhoods, the latter are unconventional areas. Since the Section 421 buildings are in residential neighborhoods, it is to be expected that their tenants would remark on the neighborhood in ways most similar to converted building residents who live in conventional areas. While this is sometimes the case, the differences are slight, and the similarities among all three groups are more noticeable. Particularly remarkable is the high and nearly equal proportion of respondents in each of the three groups who say that no city services are necessary. This suggests an acceptance of the quality of delivery of city services by a substantial number of tenants in all neighborhoods. In the unconventional areas, where the fewest services are provided, the tenants' satisfaction with the converted units or lofts seems to offset many of the dissatisfactions with neighborhood facilities.

Although there are quite pronounced differences among the three types of dwelling units being discussed, thus far there have not been substantial differences in the way tenants remark about the units or their neighborhoods. It is possible that the tenants themselves form a relatively homogeneous group and that their

EXHIBIT III-3

COMMENTS ABOUT NEIGHBORHOODS MADE BY RESIDENTS

CATEGORY	Manhattan Section 421 Buildings	CONVERTED BUILDINGS	
		Conventional Beighborhoods	Unconventional Neighborhoods
Importance of Proximity to Necessities[1]			
Food Shopping	4.4	4.7	4.4
Laundry Facilities	4.4	4.7	4.0
Dry Cleaning	3.9	4.1	3.3
Hardware/Houseware Store	2.7	3.6	3.7
Bank	3.5	3.9	3.9
Luncheonette	2.6	3.1	2.7
Library	2.6	3.2	3.1
Comments About the Neighborhood			
Positive			
Safe, Quiet, Friendly, Clean	31.7%	25.1%	23.1%
Convenient	14.9	15.2	3.7
Interesting, Varied, Lively	17.1	20.1	19.5
Known as a Good Neighborhood	9.8	--	--
Negative			
Very Noisy	9.8	0.9	7.4
Dirty, Attracts Undesirables	8.9	6.7	7.9
City Services in Need of Improvement			
Nothing Necessary	38.7%	35.0%	35.5%
Trash Collection	14.9	10.3	18.5
Street Cleaning & Repair	14.0	19.2	16.1
Recreation Facilities	7.9	5.1	6.2
Public Transportation	7.9	6.4	2.4
Police Protection	5.8	8.5	4.3

Note: [1]The ratings are based on a scale from 1 to 5, where 5 is very important and 1 is very unimportant.

Source: CUPR Survey of Residents of Section 421 Buildings; CUPR Survey of Residents of Converted Buildings.

remarks bespeak a shared viewpoint, or it is possible that all three types of units, different though they are from one another, are so much more different from other rental units available in the city that the tenants' remarks are founded more on comparisons with other rental units than on the specific qualities unique to the lofts, the converted apartments, or the Section 421 apartments. Information is available from the two surveys that can help determine how homogeneous a group is formed by the tenants of the three types of units.

PERSONAL CHARACTERISTICS OF THE TENANTS

Exhibit III-4 summarizes the personal characteristics of residents of Section 421 buildings, of converted apartments, and of lofts. Where it has been possible to find, New York City data is also shown on this exhibit for ease of comparison.

Although the residents of all three types of units are considerably younger than typical New York City renters, people who live in converted apartments are the youngest. A male head of the household occurs in converted apartments and lofts approximately as often as in renter households throughout the city, but there is an unusually high proportion of female-headed households in Section 421 buildings. While there is a much lower proportion of married people living in all three kinds of apartments than there is in the city as a whole, the lowest incidence of married couples is in converted apartments. The largest households and the highest proportions of households with children are to be found in lofts. And the measures of New York City affiliation are quite similar for residents of lofts, of converted apartments, and of Section 421 units.

The residents of lofts, converted apartments, and Section 421 units are so much better educated than average New York City residents that the differences in achievement among residents of the three types of units are of little importance. In New York City, only 10.6 of the population has completed college; however, 80.5 percent of loft residents, 69.2 percent of converted apartment residents, and 77.7 percent of Section 421 residents have equivalent attainments. Aside from the extremely high proportion of artists

EXHIBIT III-4

PERSONAL CHARACTERISTICS OF RESIDENTS

CATEGORY	NEW YORK CITY[1] Total	Manhattan Section 421 Buildings n = 389	CONVERTED BUILDINGS Converted Apartments n = 278	Residential Lofts n = 224
Age of Household Head				
Less than 20 years	N.A.	0.0%	1.8%	0.9%
20-29 years		34.7	50.4	29.7
30-39 years		42.0	33.9	48.4
40-49 years		9.2	10.2	13.2
50-59 years		7.0	2.6	6.4
60 years and over		7.0	1.1	1.4
Median Age	44.4 years (1975)	33.6 years	29.6 years	34.0 years
Sex of Household Head	(1975)			
Male	66.3%	56.5%	62.9%	67.3%
Female	33.7	43.5	36.7	32.7
Marital Status of Household Head	(1970)			
Single	34.9%	48.5%	63.7%	47.9%
Married	49.5	39.0	27.1	39.1
(Separated)	(5.6)	(4.6)	(4.4)	(9.3)
Divorced	5.0	8.9	8.8	11.2
Widowed	10.6	3.5	0.4	1.9
Schooling Completed by Household Head	(1970)			
0-7 grades	19.6%	0.0%	0.0%	0.0%
8-11 grades	33.5	0.5	1.4	0.5
Completed High School	28.3	7.6	5.8	3.2
Some College or Post-High School	8.1	14.1	23.6	15.8
4 or More Years of College	10.6	77.7	69.2	80.5

(Continued)

EXHIBIT III-4 *(continued)*

PERSONAL CHARACTERISTICS OF RESIDENTS

CATEGORY	*NEW YORK CITY*[1] *Total*	*Manhattan Section 421 Buildings n = 389*	*CONVERTED BUILDINGS* *Converted Apartments n = 278*	*Residential Lofts n = 224*
Occupation of Household Head[2]	(1970)			
Professional or Technical	13.6%	41.7%	38.2%	33.2%
Manager, Administrator or Proprietor	7.8	26.0	21.3	18.7
Artist	2.1	8.8	15.7	35.0
Sales Worker	7.3	9.9	9.7	3.7
Service Worker	12.3	2.2	6.4	1.9
Clerical	27.1	4.4	3.7	2.3
Student	--	2.5	2.6	0.9
Craftsman, Foreman	10.2	1.1	0.7	1.4
Operative	15.0	0.3	0.4	0.9
Laborer	3.3	0.3	0.4	0.5
Other	1.3	2.8	0.7	1.4
Citizenship of Household Head				
United States		81.0%	90.6%	90.5%
Foreign	N.A.	19.0	9.4	9.5
People in the Household	(1975)			
1 person	33.7%	44.9%	42.9%	29.4%
2 persons	30.5	42.5	48.4	48.2
3 persons	15.2	10.1	8.1	14.2
4 or more persons	20.6	2.4	0.7	8.2
Median	2.0 persons	1.6 persons	1.7 persons	2.1 persons

(Continued)

EXHIBIT III-4 *(continued)*

PERSONAL CHARACTERISTICS OF RESIDENTS

CATEGORY	NEW YORK CITY[1] Total	Manhattan Section 421 Buildings n = 389	CONVERTED BUILDINGS Converted Apartments n = 278	Residential Lofts n = 224
Percentage of Households with Children	N.A.	13.0%	6.8%	20.5%
Type of Tenure	(1975)			
Own	27.5%	--	--	37.2%
Rent	72.5	100.0%	100.0%	62.8
New York City Affiliation				
Born in NYC		40.8%	39.9%	38.2%
Went to Grammar School or High School in NYC	N.A.	33.5	26.4	28.5
Went to College in NYC		47.8	37.8	39.1
Household Income[2]	(1975)			
Less than $5,000	29.0%	1.8%	3.5%	7.8%
$ 5,000 - $ 9,999	29.4	2.7	6.9	5.4
$10,000 - $14,999	19.7	9.7	16.9	16.7
$15,000 - $19,999		13.7	17.7	13.7
$20,000 - $24,999		18.2	16.9	14.2
$25,000 - $29,999	21.9	14.6	12.3	13.7
$30,000 - $34,999		10.9	8.5	7.8
More than $35,000		28.3	17.3	20.6
Median	$8,395	$26,302	$21,479	$22,253

(Continued)

EXHIBIT III-4 *(continued)*

PERSONAL CHARACTERISTICS OF RESIDENTS

CATEGORY	*NEW YORK CITY*[1] *Total*	*Manhattan Section 421 Buildings n = 389*	*CONVERTED BUILDINGS* Converted Apartments n = 278	*CONVERTED BUILDINGS* Residential Lofts n = 224
Full-Time Job Holders in Household				
0		6.7%	10.9%	13.9%
1		59.2	58.5	46.4
2	N.A.	29.7	30.2	36.1
3 or more		4.5	0.4	3.6

Notes: [1]When indicated, New York City figures are either for the city population as a whole in 1970, or for renter households in 1975.

[2]The category "artist," which is normally included in the totals for professional/technical workers, has been disaggregated for comparative purposes.

[3]These income figures are from the U.S. Bureau of the Census, 1975, New York City Housing and Vacancy Survey as reported in Sternlieb and Hughes, Housing and Economic Reality. For each of these categories, the percentages are of those households which reported incomes. In the 1975 survey, 29 percent of the renters did not report their income; in the Section 421 Survey, 14 percent did not report; and in the Converted Building Survey, 7.5 percent of the residents would not reveal their income. Numbers may not total 100 percent due to rounding.

Source: CUPR Survey of Residents of 421 Buildings, October 1977; CUPR Survey of Residents of Converted Buildings, August-September, 1977; U.S. Bureau of the Census, Detail Population Characteristics, Part 34, New York; George Sternlieb and James Hughes, Housing and Economic Reality (New Brunswick, N.J., 1976).

living in lofts, the occupations pursued by residents of all three types of units are quite similar, and are markedly different from those pursued by all New York City residents. For example, the highly-skilled jobs (professional/technical, artist, manager, administrator, proprietor) are held by 23.5 percent of all New Yorkers; however, they are held by 76.5 percent of Section 421 residents, 75.2 percent of converted apartment residents, and 86.9 percent of loft residents.

It follows from the occupations of the residents of Section 421 buildings and converted buildings that the household incomes would be high. Although the Section 421 households earn the most, the incomes of households in converted apartments and in lofts are at least twice the citywide median of $9,255.

From all these statistics it can be seen that converted apartments house slightly younger people pursuing slightly lower-level occupations and earning slightly less money than the residents of Section 421 apartments and lofts. In part this is probably due to the difference in expenditures each type of unit requires. Although lofts and converted apartments cost about the same in monthly rent, the lofts usually require an investment that averages $7,100; and the Section 421 apartments cost 28 percent more per month than converted apartments.

The most noteworthy point to be made about the foregoing personal characteristics of residents of Section 421 buildings, converted apartments, and lofts is that the ways in which the residents differ from one another are small compared to how they all differ from residents of New York City in general. In fact, when considering personal characteristics, only the high incidence of artists living in lofts pronouncedly differentiates the residents of the three new types of housing.

There are other characteristics which may distinguish among the residents of Section 421 units, lofts, and converted apartments. The first group of these characteristics is manifestations of satisfaction. Exhibit III-5 compares the responses to questions about satisfaction made by residents of the three types of dwellings.

EXHIBIT III-5

LEVELS OF SATISFACTION

INDICATOR	Manhattan Section 421 Buildings	CONVERTED BUILDINGS: Converted Apartments	CONVERTED BUILDINGS: Residential Lofts
Satisfaction - on a scale from 1 to 5, on which 5 is very satisfied.	3.9	4.0	4.0
Respondents who would choose to live in the unit again.	74.9%	74.8%	89.4%
Of those who would not choose unit again, the housing type preferred:			
suburban housing	31.8%	11.3%	4.5%
larger unit	27.3	25.8	22.7
brownstone or townhouses	18.2	13.6	20.1
converted building	12.1	22.6	27.3
more luxurious building	4.5	6.5	0.0
other	6.1	20.2	25.4

Source: CUPR Survey of Residents of Section 421 Buildings, October 1977; CUPR Survey of Residents of Converted Buildings, August-September, 1977.

Although the level of satisfaction reported by residents does not vary significantly according to type of residence, the lofts are much more satisfying as measured by the high percentage of residents who would choose to live in a loft again. There is no appreciable difference between the number of residents in converted apartments and in Section 421 units who would choose their unit again. The respondents who said they would not again choose their unit were asked what kind of residence they would prefer. A very high percentage of those in Section 421 apartments preferred suburban housing; those in lofts and converted apartments mentioned other housing alternatives in New York City much more often. Perhaps residents of Section 421 units see these apartments as the ultimate alternative in New York City - new buildings, good location - and if satisfaction with these units pales, the most likely alternative would be something out of the city. People living in converted apartments and lofts do not view their unit as the ultimate choice available, and can imagine living elsewhere in the city.

A better sense of this difference among residents can be gotten from their responses to questions about inducement to stay in New York City. The people who have been in the city for the longest time are those living in lofts; the preponderance of those who have been in New York City less than five years live in converted apartments (see Exhibit III-6). Similarly, lofts house the greatest percentage of people whose former residence was in New York City. For newcomers to the city, the Section 421 buildings appear to be the most attractive, since 45 percent of the residents most recently lived outside the city. The converted apartments house the highest percentage of residents who have lived in the city less than five years, but many of these tenants have lived in at least one other New York City location before choosing the converted unit.

The residents of Section 421 apartments feel the least attachment to the city. They plan to stay in their unit for the shortest period (2.4 years), and compared to the residents of converted apartments and lofts, a high percentage have considered moving to the suburbs and a high percentage would have left New York City if a similar apartment had not been available.

EXHIBIT III-6

INDUCEMENT TO STAY IN NEW YORK CITY

INDICATOR	*Manhattan Section 421 Buildings*	*CONVERTED BUILDINGS*	
		Converted Apartments	*Residential Lofts*
Length of Residence in NYC			
Less than 5 years	38.8%	53.8%	32.5%
5-9 years	23.9	19.1	17.9
10 years or more	37.3	27.1	49.6
Location of Previous Residence			
New York City	55.0%	62.3%	73.3%
New York City Metropolitan Region[1]	8.7	6.6	4.5
Tri-State Region[2]	6.4	11.4	5.9
Other U.S.	21.6	13.1	14.0
Foreign	7.9	6.6	2.3
At the Time Respondent Decided to Move into Current Unit, Considered Moving to the Suburbs	16.3%	13.8%	13.8%
Length of Time Respondent Plans to Stay in Unit	2.4 years	3 years	8 years
Would Have Left the City if Similar Unit Had Not Been Available	12.8%	8%	8%
If Rent or Maintenance Fee Doubled, Would Leave the City	22.9%	16.7%	16.7%

Notes: [1]The New York City Metropolitan Region is the 22 county region as defined by the Port Authority and Regional Plan Association, excluding the five boroughs of N.Y.C.
[2]The Tri-State Region is New York, New Jersey and Connecticut, except for New York City and the Metropolitan Region.

Totals may not equal 100 percent because of rounding.

Source: CUPR Survey of Residents of Section 421 Buildings, October 1977; CUPR Survey of Residents of Converted Buildings, August-September 1977.

Residents of lofts feel the greatest attachment to New York City, and plan to stay in their lofts an average of eight years. Converted buildings in general, both the ones containing lofts and those with converted apartments, house only a small percentage of residents who considered moving to the suburbs or who would have left the city if similar units had not been available.

From this information about satisfaction and inducement, it seems credible that the residents of Section 421 buildings are more likely to view their apartments as the best and last alternative to leaving the city than are the residents of lofts and converted apartments. The latter two types of units house people more likely to remain in the city if they become dissatisfied with their unit. However, the large majority of residents of all three types of units have neither considered moving to the suburbs nor would have left the city had a similar unit not been available.

SUMMARY

This chapter has compared the characteristics of the two most important new housing options available in New York City. The most significant results of this comparison are listed below.

1. There are significant differences between Section 421 buildings in Manhattan and in the other four boroughs. In addition, all the converted buildings under study are in Manhattan. Therefore, all the comparisons are made between buildings located in Manhattan.

2. All Section 421 buildings (in Manhattan) are new, and most of them contain more than 250 apartments. The converted buildings are older; their architecture represents the fashion of their day and heralds their former commercial or industrial use. Converted apartments are in buildings with 130 units; lofts are typically in buildings with only 12 units.

3. On the average, lofts contain 2100 square feet and have median monthly rents of $392; converted apartments have only 610 square feet and median rents of $393; and Section 421 units contain 875 square feet and the median monthly cost is $506. The monthly price per square foot is about the same for the latter two types of dwellings ($.58 for Section 421 units, $.64 for converted apartments), and nearly three times the price for lofts ($.19 per square foot per month). The citywide median rent was $171 in 1975.

4. The largest proportion of residents of all three types of units appears to be able to choose a place to live in New York City based on some physical quality of a particular unit. Except for artists' requiring large spaces at low prices per square foot, most of the residents appear to be able to afford to live wherever the amenities and the location suit them.

5. Although the residents of all three types of units are considerably younger than typical New York City renters, the people living in converted apartments are the youngest. The comparative median ages are: Section 421 units, 33.6 years; lofts, 34.0 years; converted apartments, 29.6 years; and for New York City, the median age for renters was 44.4 years in 1975.

6. The residents of lofts, converted apartments, and Section 421 units are so much better educated than average New York City residents that the differences among the residents of new types of units are of little importance. In New York City, only 10.6 percent of the population has completed college; however, 80.5 percent of loft residents, 69.2 percent of converted apartment residents, and 77.7 percent of Section 421 residents have equivalent attainments.

7. Aside from the high percentage of artists residing in lofts, the occupations pursued by residents in all three types of units are quite similar, and markedly different from

those pursued by typical New York City residents. For example, the highly-skilled jobs (professional/technical, artist, manager, administrator, proprietor) are held by 23.5 percent of all New Yorkers; however, the same type of jobs are held by 76.5 percent of Section 421 residents, 75.2 percent of converted apartment residents, and 86.9 percent of loft residents.

8. Median household incomes are likewise much higher than for typical New York City households ($9,255). Loft households earn $22,253, converted apartment households earn $21,479, and Section 421 households earn $24,268.

9. The most noteworthy point to be made about these comparisons of residents of Section 421 units, converted apartments, and lofts, is that the ways in which they differ from one another are small compared to how they all differ from residents of New York City in general.

10. The levels of satisfaction do not vary noticeably among the residents of the three new types of housing. However, the residents of lofts intend to stay in their units much longer than the other residents, and nearly all of the loft residents would choose to live there again.

11. Nearly a third of the dissatisfied residents of Section 421 housing intend to look for suburban housing next, implying that they consider their unit the ultimate alternative in New York City, and that dissatisfaction forces them to look outside the city. For the most part, dissatisfied residents of both types of units in converted buildings intend to look elsewhere in the city for a new unit.

12. Despite the dissatisfaction evident in point 11 above, the large majority of residents of all three types of units have neither considered moving to the suburbs nor would have left the city had a similar unit not been available.

13. Residents of lofts feel the greatest attachment to New York City. Few of these residents either considered moving to the suburbs or would have left the city if a similar unit had not been available.

14. By encouraging conversion and new construction, New York City is adding attractive housing options to its stock of dwelling units. These are providing homes for young, well-educated, highly paid tenants, the residents who make important contributions of their skills and their spending to the city's economy.

15. It could well be argued that continued production of all three types of units should be encouraged in order to accommodate the diverse tastes of these valuable residents.

The photograph below shows a conventional residential neighborhood where it is apparently pleasant to stroll; the picture on the opposing page is of an unconvention area where a pedestrian would have to dodge loading docks and endure truck noise

Frank Gradilo

Frank Gradilon

Chapter 4

COMMUTERS TO NEW YORK CITY—POTENTIAL CITY RESIDENTS?

INTRODUCTION

After years of watching middle class families move out of cities into suburban areas, years during which cities seemed to be able only to rely on the very rich and the very poor to continue to be residents, observers find evidence that there are new population trends. Some members of the middle class appear to be moving back to the cities, and other middle class residents are choosing to stay in the central city rather than move to the suburbs.[1] Although the most noticeable migration patterns continue to be movements away from central cities, there are four factors which contribute to the small reverse movement that scholars have been able to discern.

First, increased fuel costs and the uncertain future quantities of fuel have improved the locational advantages of central-city areas. Second, environmental concerns have constrained suburban development by making it more difficult and costly than it has been before. Third, the cost of constructing and servicing new housing has increased extravagantly, making new suburban homes less attractive to homebuyers and taxpayers. And finally, the personal characteristics of metropolitan populations have changed; there are larger proportions of childless and single-person households than before, households for which better schools and improved play areas are irrelevant. Of more interest are jobs, entertainment, and other cultural divertissements.

In short, both demand and supply characteristics for residential locations have changed, and the result seems to many observers to be that central cities will enjoy a new attractiveness to middle-income people.

The Urban Land Institute predicts that those who return to the cities because of these reasons will demand lower residential densities than have typically been available in urban core areas.[2] This prediction is based on the assumption that the returning population will want to replicate low density suburban living while taking advantage of the big city environment.

This prediction, and indeed the discernment of the increasing attractiveness of central cities to middle class citizens, acknowledges the small numbers of people yet involved. But it is argued that the combination of the four factors cited above is sufficiently potent that a real change is imaginable.

If it is the case that the four reasons are compelling, and that the returning citizens will demand lower density residential areas than typical of central cities, then converted buildings would seem eminently attractive to people moving back to the city. The recycled buildings, particularly those with lofts, offer floor areas equivalent to suburban houses, and they are in buildings of a small scale, buildings which shelter far fewer households than the high-rise apartments that provide the large part of the city's housing options for higher income residents.

This chapter describes the results of a survey of people who commute to New York City. The survey was conducted in order to find what interest there is among commuters in moving to the city, and more particularly to discover how attractive the converted buildings are to suburbanites.

In 1970, the last date for which there is definitive data, there were 609,566 people who commuted to New York City to work.[3] While it would be most desirable to choose a sample representative of all commuters, inclusive lists such as the rolls of New York City nonresident income taxpayers were kept confidential by the State. Therefore, the study was confined to people who commute to New York City on railroads, approximately a third of all commuters.[4] It is possible only to speculate about the differences among rail, bus and automobile commuters because definitive data are simply not available. Therefore, this study can only be understood to speak about people who commute to New York City by rail. (A description of the methodology appears in Appendix B.)

The results will be presented first for the entire sample of railroad commuters. A more robust understanding of the data will be possible in the second part of this chapter which describes significant variations in the data that can be found when age, the presence of children, state of residence, and plans to move to New York City are taken into account. Included will be a characterization of the commuters who reported that they would like to live in a converted building.

ALL COMMUTERS

Personal Characteristics of All Rail Commuters

The median age of people who use the railroad to commute to New York City is 43.8 years. Typically, the commuter is very well educated (75 percent have at least completed college), works in a highly-skilled occupation (75 percent have professional or technical jobs, or are managers, administrators or proprietors), works in Manhattan (96 percent of the rail commuters), and is very well paid (median annual household income is $36,046). The suburbanite is characteristically white (only 1.5 percent of the rail commuters are black), married (90 percent), and lives in a household of four people. Usually the commuter is the only full-time job holder in the household (30 percent of the households have more than one full-time worker), and has at least one child younger than 18 years (67 percent of the households).

The railroad commuters live in detached, single-family homes (such structures house 92 percent of the commuters) which they own (80 percent of all commuters). The median monthly mortgage payment, including property tax, is $428. Nearly 60 percent of the suburban residents bought their house more than five years ago; the median price paid for the suburban house is nearly $45,000. For those who rent their suburban residence, the median rent is $329 per month. Utility payments average $136 per month for owners and $51 for renters.

The above characteristics comport with how one might expect to describe upper middle class suburban residents. Of these commuters, 55 percent have lived as adults in New York City (i.e., they lived in a household separate from that of their parents). The reasons that these former New Yorkers give for having left the city are predominantly that the person wanted to own a house (27 percent), wanted to enjoy suburban amenities such as fresh air or cleanliness (27 percent), or wanted to move for reasons that are related to having children, such as private yards for play or better schools (19 percent). Only 4 percent of these former residents of the city cited the fear of crime or the poor city services as reasons for their move. In short, the large majority of one-time New Yorkers wanted to enjoy the life available in New York City's suburbs, a life they believed could not be found in the city.

The sample of railroad commuters spends an average of two and a half hours each day getting to and returning from work. However, this sacrifice of time does not seem to weigh much in a commuter's assessment of his contentment. When asked to rate satisfaction, using a scale from 1 to 5 on which 5 is very satisfied, the commuters reported an average rating of 4.2. This high rating does not vary when the respondents are divided into two groups, those who spend more than two hours a day commuting and those who spend less than two hours a day. Contentment is also revealed by the commuters' saying that they intend to stay in their current residence an average of 12 years.

To get a sense of how the commuters spend their leisure time, the respondents were asked to rate five different leisure time activities according to how important each was to them. Most important is outdoor recreation (3.6), next is relaxing at home (3.4), followed by going out to eat (3.1) and going to movies and plays (2.8), and least important is going to museums (2.1). The two most important activities certainly do not require going to New York City, and going out to eat or to movies can easily occur in suburban areas.

Attitudes of All Rail Commuters Toward New York City

The rail commuters were asked several questions intended to illuminate their attitudes toward New York City in general and toward living there in particular. The specific questions asked were:

1. How many times each year do you have dinner, see a play, watch a movie, etc., in New York City?

2. How many times a month do you go out to dinner, see a play, etc., when you do not go into New York City?

3. Would you like to live in New York City?

4. Do you plan to move to New York City?

5. Have you heard about the conversion of loft and warehouse space into apartments? If so, would you like to live in one?

6. If you had to move to New York City next year, which borough would you prefer? What kind of housing would you choose, and how much would you be willing to pay for it?

7. What do you most enjoy about the city, and what do you dislike the most about the city?

8. If your rent (if owned-property taxes) and utility bills were to double in the next year, what would you do?

On the average, the commuters go to New York City once a month for some type of entertainment. For similar entertainment available in the suburbs, they go out about three times a month. For most of the commuters, working in New York City and being entertained there once a month apparently is sufficient exposure to the city, as evidenced by only 22 percent of these suburbanites saying that they would like to live in the city.

Only 11 percent of the total sample plan to move to New York City, and the plans are fairly far in the future. The positive respondents estimate the move to occur in about eight and a half years. The reasons for planning to move are primarily because children will have grown up so that a suburban location is no longer necessary (40 percent), or because the head of the household wants to live closer to where he works (33 percent). Those who plan to move to New York City intend to live in Manhattan (91 percent), and would prefer to live in high-rise apartments (60 percent) or brownstones (17 percent). Only 2 percent of these commuters said they would choose to live in a converted building.

The people who do not plan to move to New York City, nearly 90 percent of the commuters, were asked why they had no such plans and also were asked if there was anything the city could do that would make them want to move there. The reasons given for not planning to move to the city are its lack of suburban amenities (23 percent), a general dislike of the city (17 percent), the city's being unfit as a place to rear children (15 percent), the city's being too crowded (12 percent), and the respondent's desire to own a house (12 percent). Less frequently mentioned are the fear of crime (7 percent), the city's being too expensive (7 percent), and dissatisfaction with specific city supplied services such as garbage collection (4 percent). These reasons apparently are immutable, since nearly two-thirds of those who have no plans to move to the city say that there is nothing the city could do to make them change their minds. More sanguine commuters say that they would move to the city if the crime rate were lower (10 percent), or if the city were cleaned up (9 percent). A few respondents say that a lower cost of living (6.3 percent) or better schools (3.5 percent) would induce them to move to New York City.

In the introduction to this chapter it was posited that because of the low densities and large apartments to be found in converted buildings, these recycled structures would be an attractive housing option to people who move from suburban locales to the city. As a test of this speculation the rail commuters were asked if they had heard of buildings being converted to residential use, and those who were aware of the conversions were asked whether they would like to live in one. Approximately two-thirds of the commuters know about buildings being converted to residential use. Of these, less than 20 percent say they would like to live in a converted building. The desirable qualities are reported to be the large, unconventional, or flexible features of converted space (12 percent), the convenience of living closer to work and to activity (4 percent) and the neighborhood ambience found where converted buildings are sited (2 percent). The reasons for not wanting to live in converted structures are that the commuter is happy in his current residence (30 percent), that the converted spaces are too small or are not desirable for families (25 percent), that the neighborhoods are not pleasant (14 percent) or that the life style associated with conversions is not appealing. For most commuters the recycled buildings do not compete with suburban circumstances. A later section of this report will consider the characteristics of people who would like to live in a converted building.

Having asked about the rail commuters' preferences and plans, the interviewers next gave a series of hypothetical questions. The commuters were requested to consider what they would do if they had to move to New York City in the next year. Specifically, they were asked which borough they would choose, what type of housing they would prefer, and how much rent (or monthly payment) they could imagine having to pay.

Manhattan was chosen by most respondents (68 percent), and is considered much more desirable than all other boroughs combined: Queens (17 percent), Staten Island (8 percent), Brooklyn (5 percent), and the Bronx (2 percent). High-rise apartment buildings are the most desirable type of housing (chosen by 32 percent of the commuters), next are detached houses (28 percent; most likely this is the choice of those respondents who would like to live in boroughs other than Manhattan), brownstones or townhouses (29 percent) and garden apartments (9 percent). Only 1 percent of the respondents mentioned a converted building. This implies that even the respondents who said they would like to live in converted buildings do not seriously or consciously consider them as places to live. Finally, the commuters expected that they would have to pay a median rent of $479 per month for housing in the city, a figure approximately 12 percent higher than their reported monthly cost of housing in the suburbs exclusive of utilities.

The rail commuters were asked what they most enjoyed about New York City. The three most enjoyable aspects are the cultural activities available (37 percent), the excitement or ambience of the city (23 percent), and the recreation and entertainment to be found (18 percent). What is most interesting about this pattern of responses is that it does not vary according to the earlier reported ranking of importance of leisure time activities. For example, people for whom going to museums is not very important do not mention the enjoyment of these cultural activities any less often than people who rate going to museums as most important. Similarly, the importance of each of the other leisure time activities does not imply a different sense of what is most enjoyable about the city. A possible explanation is that for many commuters it is important that in the city there be cultural activities, first run movies, and excellent restaurants, whether or not the commuter himself finds any of these particularly important. This implies that the commuter has a sense of what New York City should make available, and that this sense is not much affected by personal predilection.

Rail commuters also were asked what they disliked the most about New York City. Most frequently mentioned are the filth and pollution found in the city (27 percent), the crime (25 percent), and the crowding or congestion of the city (22 percent). No other complaint was made by more than 5 percent of the respondents.

Finally, the commuters were asked to consider what they would do if their rent (or property taxes) and utility bills were to double in the next year. While 57 percent of the respondents siad they would pay the increase, 14 percent would move to another New York City suburb, 13 percent would move to a different area entirely, and 3 percent would move to New York City. Surely the most noteworthy point to be made is that most rail commuters believe that suburban satisfactions are worth more than even a greatly increased cost of living in the suburbs.

DIFFERENT SETS OF COMMUTERS

The discussion thus far has been about the railroad commuters considered as a homogeneous group. This has provided a sense of the group, but it is possible to get more information about attitudes toward New York City when the group is divided into categories according to distinguishing characteristics. This section of the chapter will consider several subgroups, based on whether the commuter has children, the commuter's age, the state the commuter lives in, whether the commuter plans to move to New York City, and whether the commuter would like to live in a converted building.

Subgroups of Commuters: Personal Characteristics

Exhibit IV-1 summarizes the personal characteristics for all railroad commuters, and for the commuters when they are arranged in subgroups. The notation "same as universe" that is shown for many questions means that there was no significant difference among or between subgroup members, and that the response for all commuters is appropriate. For example, the age distributions of the household heads for New York State residents is not significantly different from that for household heads living in New Jersey and Connecticut.

The most noticeable information to be learned from Exhibit V-1 is how homogeneous a group the commuters are with respect to personal characteristics. For example, although the typical commuter with children is younger than the typical childless commuter, the age does not vary among the states, among the people who do and do not plan to move to New York City, nor among the people who would and would not like to live in a converted building. Similarly, marital status, household size, and number of workers in the household vary only when age of the household head or the presence of children are used to differentiate among the commuters. The variations are fairly predictable. For example, older people are less likely to have many children younger than 18 years, and this is shown in the smaller average number of children found in households headed by someone at least 40 years old. However, the same older people are more likely to have children at least 18 years old (and aging parents) living with them, and this accounts for the average household size being larger for older commuters.

EXHIBIT IV-1

PERSONAL CHARACTERISTICS OF RAILROAD COMMUTERS

Characteristic	*All Railroad Commuters*	*Children in Household*		*Age of Head of Household*		*State of Residence*			*Plans to Move to New York*		*Would Like to Live in a Converted Building*[1]	
		None	*Some*	*<40 yrs.*	*≥40 yrs.*	*New York*	*New Jersey*	*Connecticut*	*Yes*	*No*	*Yes*	*No*
	n = 678	*n = 214*	*n = 457*	*n = 253*	*n = 416*	*n = 428*	*n = 168*	*n = 82*	*n = 70*	*n = 595*	*n = 74*	*n = 344*
Age of Household Head												
<20 years	-	-	-	-	-							
20-29 years	7.0%	14.8%	3.1%	18.6%	-							
30-34 years	12.7	10.0	14.1	33.6	-							
35-39 years	18.1	6.7	23.4	47.8	-	Same as Universe[2]			Same as Universe		Same as Universe	
40-49 years	32.7	14.8	41.1	-	52.6%							
50-59 years	23.5	37.8	17.0	-	37.7							
60 years or older	6.0	15.8	1.3		9.6							
Median Age	43.7 yrs.	51 yrs.	42.3 yrs.									
Maritan Status												
Single	9.7%	16.8%	6.4%	7.1%	12.5%							
Married	87.9	78.1	92.5	92.5	84.1							
(Separated)	(0.1)	(0.5)	(0.0)	(0.0)	(0.2)	Same as Universe			Same as Universe		Same as Universe	
Divorced	0.7	1.4	0.4	0.4	1.0							
Widowed	1.6	3.7	0.7	0.4	2.4							
People in Household												
1 person	1.8%	5.6%	-	2.4%	2.2%							
2 persons	19.3	60.1	0.2%	21.4	17.8							
3 persons	16.4	15.0	17.1	18.7	14.7							
4 persons	34.2	14.1	43.5	40.9	30.4	Same as Universe			Same as Universe		Same as Universe	
5 persons	17.5	5.2	23.2	12.3	20.7							
6 persons	6.7	-	9.8	3.6	8.7							
7 persons	2.2	-	3.3	0.4	2.7							
8 or more persons	1.9	-	2.8	0.4	2.9							
Average Size of Household	3.9 persons	2.5 persons	4.5 persons	3.5 persons	4.0 persons							

(continued)

EXHIBIT IV-1 *(continued)*

PERSONAL CHARACTERISTICS OF RAILROAD COMMUTERS

Characteristic	*All Railroad Commuters*	*Children in Household*		*Age of Head of Household*		*State of Residence*			*Plans to Move to New York*		*Would Like to Live in a Converted Building*[1]	
	n = 678	*None* *n = 214*	*Some* *n = 457*	*<40 yrs.* *n = 253*	*≥40 yrs.* *n = 416*	*New York* *n = 428*	*New Jersey* *n = 168*	*Connecticut* *n = 82*	*Yes* *n = 70*	*No* *n = 595*	*Yes* *n = 74*	*No* *n = 344*
Occupation of Head of Household												
Professional or Technical	35.8%	34.0%	36.3%								40.3%	35.5%
Manager, Administrator or Proprietor	36.7	32.1	39.0								26.4	37.9
Sales Worker	16.7	16.3	17.1								22.2	16.6
Craftsman, Foreman	2.9	4.8	2.0								4.2	2.7
Clerical	2.3	3.3	1.8	Same as Universe		Same as Universe			Same as Universe		1.4	1.2
Operative	0.2	0.5	-								1.4	0.0
Laborer	0.2	0.5	-								0.0	3.0
Artist	3.0	4.3	2.2								2.8	3.3
Service Worker	2.0	2.9	1.6								-	3.0
Other	0.5	1.5	-								1.4	-
Income[3]												
under $5,000	0.2%			-	0.3%	-	0.7%	-	-	0.2%		
$ 5,000 - $ 9,999	-			-	-	-	-	-	-	-		
$10,000 - $14,999	4.9			2.6%	1.5	3.0%	-	-	3.4%	1.8		
$15,000 - $19,999	6.2			7.8	5.3	6.1	8.5	2.9%	-	7.2	Same as Universe	
$20,000 - $24,999	10.4	Same as Universe		12.2	9.4	12.1	10.6	2.9	5.1	11.5		
$25,000 - $29,999	13.1			14.3	11.7	12.1	17.0	8.7	5.1	13.9		
$30,000 - $34,999	15.5			17.4	14.4	14.9	15.6	18.8	13.6	15.9		
$35,000 - $39,999	12.9			15.2	11.1	14.3	9.9	10.1	11.9	12.5		
$40,000 - $49,999	13.8			10.1	16.1	13.2	15.6	13.0	13.6	13.7		
$50,000 or more	26.1			20.0	30.2	24.2	22.0	43.5	47.5	23.3		
Median Income	$36,046			$39,309	$38,333	$35,629	$34,230	$45,076	$48,013	$34,841		

(continued)

EXHIBIT IV-1 *(continued)*

PERSONAL CHARACTERISTICS OF RAILROAD COMMUTERS

Characteristic	*All Railroad Commuters*	*Children in Household*		*Age of Head of Household*		*State of Residence*			*Plans to Move to New York*		*Would Like to Live in a Converted Building*[1]	
		None	*Some*	*<40 yrs.*	*≥40 yrs.*	*New York*	*New Jersey*	*Connecticut*	*Yes*	*No*	*Yes*	*No*
	n = 678	*n = 214*	*n = 457*	*n = 253*	*n = 416*	*n = 428*	*n = 168*	*n = 82*	*n = 70*	*n = 595*	*n = 74*	*n = 344*
Children (under 18 years old) in Household												
0 children	31.9%	100.0%	-	26.4%	34.7%	34.4%	29.8%	23.5%	Same as Universe		Same as Universe	
1 child	20.1	-	29.5%	17.6	21.6	19.4	20.2	23.5				
2 children	31.1	-	45.5	40.4	26.0	32.5	28.0	29.6				
3 children	11.8	-	17.3	11.6	11.9	9.0	18.5	12.3				
4 or more children	5.2	-	7.7	4.0	5.8	4.7	3.6	11.1				
Average number of Children	1.4	-	2.0	1.5	1.3	1.3	1.5	1.6				
Full-time Workers in Household												
None	0.1%	0.5%	-	-	0.2%	Same as Universe			Same as Universe		Same as Universe	
1 worker	66.9	43.7	77.8%	71.0%	64.6							
2 workers	27.2	46.0	18.5	28.2	26.6							
3 workers	3.4	5.6	2.4	0.4	5.1							
4 workers	1.6	2.8	1.1	0.4	2.4							
5 or more workers	0.6	1.4	0.1	-	1.0							

(continued)

EXHIBIT IV-1 *(continued)*

PERSONAL CHARACTERISTICS OF RAILROAD COMMUTERS

Characteristic	*All Railroad Commuters*	*Children in Household*		*Age of Head of Household*		*State of Residence*			*Plans to Move to New York*		*Would Like to Live in a Converted Building*[1]	
	n = 678	*None n = 214*	*Some n = 457*	*<40 yrs. n = 253*	*≥40 yrs. n = 416*	*New York n = 428*	*New Jersey n = 168*	*Connecticut n = 82*	*Yes n = 70*	*No n = 595*	*Yes n = 74*	*No n = 344*
Percentage that are American Citizens	96.7%	Same as Universe		Same as Universe		98.1%	95.2%	92.7%	Same as Universe		Same as Universe	
New York City Affiliation												
Born in New York City	49.6%	Same as Universe		Same as Universe		59.8%	33.3%	29.6%	Same as Universe		Same as Universe	
Went to Grammar School or High School in NYC	47.4%	Same as Universe		Same as Universe		57.6%	33.9%	22.0%	Same as Universe		Same as Universe	
Went to College in New York City	47.7%	Same as Universe		Same as Universe		52.6%	44.0%	29.6%	62.9%	45.9%	Same as Universe	

Notes: [1]This column reports the responses given by people who have heard of converted buildings (62.2 percent of the commuters).
[2]"Same as Universe" means that the responses among the various subgroups are not significantly different from each other, and the response shown in the column titled "All Railroad Commuters" is the appropriate figure.
[3]The percentages shown for income are proportions of the commuters who reported their income. Of the entire sample of 678 commuters, 15.5 percent would not reveal the household income.

Numbers may not total 100 percent because of rounding.

Source: CUPR Survey of Commuters who travel to New York City by rail, March 1978.

People living in New York State have slightly fewer children, on average, than residents of New Jersey and Connecticut. However, the state of residence is not a source of variation for most other personal characteristics except income and New York City affiliation. Residents of Connecticut have the largest median household incomes ($45,076), and the smallest percentage of people who were born in New York City or who went to school there. Commuters from New Jersey enjoy median household income of $34;230, nearly the same as the $35,629 reported by commuters from New York State.

The variations shown for occupations are statistically significant, but do not divide the commuters into groups that are intellectually very meaningful. White collar jobs are held by a slightly greater proportion of older commuters than by the younger group, but the small difference does not clearly demark older and younger commuters.

The personal characteristics of commuters either do not vary, or vary only in fairly predictable ways when the whole group is divided according to age, presence of children, and state of residence.

Two partitions of commuters of particular interest to this study are those who plan to move to New York City and those who would like to live in a converted building. Once again the survey results show that the personal characteristics are virtually invariant between those who would and would not like to live in a converted building.

The only personal characteristics that distinguish between commuters with and without intentions to move to New York City are median income levels and the percentage that went to college in New York City. While 63 percent of the people who plan to move to New York went to college there, this experience is common to only 46 percent of the people without plans to move to the city. But a more telling point is that the median annual income of people who intend to move to New York City is $48,013, nearly 40 percent higher than the earnings of those with no such plans ($34,841). If these plans come to pass, the city will enjoy an influx of very affluent citizens.

As for the commuters who said they would like to live in a converted building, their personal characteristics do not set tham in a group apart from all other commuters. In fact, their only trait significantly different from people who would not like to live in converted buildings is the distribution of occupations. While nearly three quarters of the people who would not enjoy a converted unit are employed in white collar jobs, two-thirds of those who view more favorably the recycled units are similarly employed. But here again, the fact of there being a statistical difference does not bespeak a compelling intellectual difference, and as Exhibit V-1 shows, the variation seems slight. The attractiveness of converted buildings to commuters does not seem to be predictable from a specific set of individual traits.

The personal characteristics of railroad commuters are essentially consistent when the whole set is divided into groups according to the state where the commuter resides, his age, whether or not he has children, his plans to move to New York City, or his being able to imagine enjoying living in a converted building. *The only particularly salient feature to surface from this sea of facts is that the people who intend to move to New York City are especially affluent.*

Subgroups of Commuters
Housing Characteristics

Exhibit IV-2 tabulates the responses that commuters made about their current housing. Once again the exhibit gives responses for all commuters and for different partitions of commuters when the answers differ significantly from one another. For example, the length of time that people have been living in their current residence is no different for those who plan to move to New York City than for those who do not.

In general, the railroad commuters have lived in their suburban residences at least five years. The most noticeable deviations from this pattern occur among respondents younger than 40 years old, and the residents of Connecticut. The former deviation is predictable; the latter means that Connecticut has recently attracted a larger portion of its commuting residents than have New York and New Jersey. Typically, people without children have lived in their residence longer than those with children, and this is probably one correlate of the age difference between the two types of households that was discussed earlier.

EXHIBIT IV-2

HOUSING CHARACTERISTICS OF RAILROAD COMMUTERS CURRENT RESIDENCE

Characteristic	All Railroad Commuters n = 678	Children in Household: None n = 214	Children in Household: Some n = 457	Age of Head of Household: <40 yrs. n = 253	Age of Head of Household: ≥40 yrs. n = 416	State of Residence: New York n = 428	State of Residence: New Jersey n = 168	State of Residence: Connecticut n = 82	Plans to Move to New York: Yes n = 70	Plans to Move to New York: No n = 595	Would Like to Live in a Converted Building[1]: Yes n = 74	Would Like to Live in a Converted Building[1]: No n = 344
Length of Time at Current Residence												
1 year or less	4.8%	6.5%	3.9%	8.7%	2.4%	1.6%	11.4%	7.3%				
1-2 years	12.7	12.1	12.9	24.2	6.5	11.2	12.0	24.4				
3-5 years	24.2	17.8	27.2	37.7	15.6	21.7	24.6	34.1	Same as Universe[2]		Same as Universe	
5 years or more	58.4	63.6	55.9	29.4	75.5	65.4	52.1	34.1				
Comparison of Current Residence to Size of Previous Residence												
Larger than previous residence	81.5%	70.7%	86.6%									
About the same	7.8	13.9	4.9	Same as Universe		Same as Universe			Same as Universe		Same as Universe	
Smaller than previous residence	10.7	15.4	8.5									
Type of Tenancy												
Own	89.2%	78.9%	94.3%	84.2%	92.5%	89.3%	85.0%	97.6%	98.6%	88.0%		
Rent	10.7	21.1	5.7	15.8	7.5	10.7	15.0	2.4	1.4	12.0	Same as Universe	
Owners												
Monthly mortgage and property tax payments	$428	$390	$441	$455	$409	$415	$395	$571	$538	$413	$495	$422
Monthly utility payments	$136	$127	$139	$125	$144	$140	$124	$139	$162	$133	$145	$142

(continued)

EXHIBIT IV-2 *(continued)*

HOUSING CHARACTERISTICS OF RAILROAD COMMUTERS CURRENT RESIDENCE

Characteristic	*All Railroad Commuters n = 678*	*Children in Household*		*Age of Head of Household*		*State of Residence*			*Plans to Move to New York*		*Would Like to Live in a Converted Building*[1]	
		None n = 214	*Some n = 457*	*<40 yrs. n = 253*	*≥40 yrs. n = 416*	*New York n = 428*	*New Jersey n = 168*	*Connecticut n = 82*	*Yes n = 70*	*No n = 595*	*Yes n = 74*	*No n = 344*
Owners (Cont'd)												
Purchase price:[3]												
less than $ 5,000	0.2%	0.8%	-	-	0.3%	0.3%	-	-	-	0.2%	-	0.4%
$ 5,000 - $ 9,999	1.3	3.3	0.6%	-	2.1	2.0	-	-	-	1.5	-	2.1
$10,000 - $14,999	3.4	6.7	1.8	-	5.6	5.3	-	-	3.8%	3.5	1.9%	3.8
$15,000 - $19,999	4.1	9.2	2.1	-	5.9	5.0	3.9%	-	-	4.7	1.9	4.2
$20,000 - $24,999	7.5	8.3	7.3	4.0%	9.8	9.9	4.9	-	1.9	8.2	7.5	8.4
$25,000 - $29,999	8.2	8.3	8.2	5.2	9.8	7.9	12.6	1.7%	7.7	8.5	5.7	8.4
$30,000 - $39,999	17.7	11.7	19.9	16.7	18.5	18.2	19.4	11.9	19.2	17.7	20.8	15.5
$40,000 - $49,999	16.4	19.2	15.5	21.8	13.2	19.2	13.6	6.8	19.2	16.2	13.2	16.0
$50,000 - $69,999	23.7	20.8	24.9	36.2	16.4	21.5	32.0	20.3	19.2	23.6	22.6	21.8
more than $70,000	17.5	11.7	19.6	16.1	18.5	10.6	13.6	59.3	28.8	15.9	26.4	19.3
Median Price	$44,634	$40,885	$46,515	$51,271	$38,919	$40,729	$46,764	>$70,000	$49,062	$43,518	$49,242	$44,500
Renters												
Monthly rent payment (including utilities)	$369	$329	$447	$351	$387	$373	$361	$290	N.A.	$359	$369	$379

(continued)

EXHIBIT IV-2 *(continued)*

HOUSING CHARACTERISTICS OF RAILROAD COMMUTERS CURRENT RESIDENCE

Characteristic	All Railroad Commuters n = 678	Children in Household: None n = 214	Children in Household: Some n = 457	Age of Head of Household: <40 yrs. n = 253	Age of Head of Household: ≥40 yrs. n = 416	State of Residence: New York n = 428	State of Residence: New Jersey n = 168	State of Residence: Connecticut n = 82	Plans to Move to New York: Yes n = 70	Plans to Move to New York: No n = 595	Would Like to Live in a Converted Building[1]: Yes n = 74	Would Like to Live in a Converted Building[1]: No n = 344
Type of Building												
Detached House	91.5%	80.3%	96.7%			91.1%	89.2%	96.3%				
Garden Apartment[4]	3.9	10.3	0.9			2.8	8.4	2.4				
Highrise Apartment	3.0	7.0	1.1	Same as Universe		4.0	1.8	-	Same as Universe		Same as Universe	
Townhouse	1.2	1.9	0.9			1.4	0.6	1.2				
Brownstone	0.3	0.5	0.2			0.5	-	-				
Other	0.1	-	0.2			0.2	-	-				
Level of Satisfaction												
(Using a scale from 1 to 5, on which 5 is very satisfied)	4.2	Same as Universe		Same as Universe		Same as Universe			3.9	4.2	3.9	4.3

Notes: [1]This column reports the responses given by people who have heard of converted buildings (62.2 percent of the commuters).
[2]Same as Universe" means that the responses among the various subgroups are not significantly different from each other, and the response shown in column titled "All Railroad Commuters" is the appropriate figure.
[3]The percentages shown are the of the respondents who revealed the price of their house; 23.2 percent of all railroad commuters who own their residence did not report its price.
[4]A garden apartment has no more than four floors, and the residents share the entrance.

Source: CUPR Survey of Commuters who travel to New York City by railroad, March 1978.

Although statistically significant differences appear among the several subgroups when an analysis is made of their responses to questions about the size of their former residence and about whether they own or rent their current home, the differences are small. The large majority of all commuters, and of any partitions of them, live in a residence larger than their previous home, and an even larger proportion own the house.

The typical monthly cost (mortgage and property tax payments) for those who own their residence is $428. Older people pay slightly less, perhaps because they bought the home several years ago; people with children pay slightly more, perhaps because the residence is larger than what childless households occupy; residents of Connecticut pay approximately 40 percent more than owners in New York and New Jersey, a percentage difference nearly equivalent to the income differential among the three states that was found earlier; people who intend to move to New York City pay 30 percent more for housing than those who do not, again an indication of the divergent income levels of the two groups; and finally, people who would like to live in a converted building pay about 18 percent more a month for housing than people uninterested in converted buildings.

Prices paid by renters vary slightly from the patterns shown for owners. For example, the older commuters pay more than the younger, and Connecticut residents pay substantially less than renters in New York and New Jersey. However, the sample size of renters is very small (73 households), and when partitioned into the various subgroups becomes so small as to be very unreliable (e.g., only two people rent a residence in Connecticut).

The type of building in which commuters make their home is almost exclusively a single-family house. As can be seen in Exhibit IV-2, there are a few deviations from this configuration, but in no instance do less than 80 percent of any subgroup live in a detached house.

Finally, the commuters were asked to rate their satisfaction using a scale from 1 to 5 on which 5 is very satisfied. In general, these particular suburbanites are well satisfied, as indicated by their rating of 4.2 (see Exhibit IV-2). This high level is invariant when the presence or absence of children is considered, when the age of the head of the household is considered, or when the state where the commuter resides is considered. However, people who intend to move to New York City and people who would like to live in converted buildings are significantly less satisfied than commuters who do not plan to move to the city or who would not like to live in converted buildings.

To summarize, the typical railroad commuter lives in an expensive house that he has owned for at least five years, that is larger than the residence where he lived most recently, and that is well satisfying to him.

Subgroups of Commuters: Leisure Time Activities

An interesting aspect of the lives of commuters can be gotten from their responses to questions about leisure time activities and preferences. As Exhibit IV-3 shows, there is little variation in the frequency that the several subgroups go to New York City for some leisure time activity. In general, commuters come to the city about once a month to spend an evening or part of a weekend. *However, people who plan to move to New York City and those who would like to live in a converted building come to the city nearly twice as often as their counterparts.* This provides a clear distinction between groups of commuters: the people most likely to report that they intend to move to New York City and those most able to imagine enjoying living in a converted building are those who come to the city often for divertissements.

The frequency that the commuters go out in the suburbs, between three and four times a month, varies little among the several partitions. As one could predict, people without children generally go out for entertainment more often than people who have youngsters. But aside from this perturbation, the pattern for leisure time is fairly regular.

Finally, Exhibit IV-3 shows how the commuters ranked various leisure time pursuits. The respondents were asked to rate each of the five activities according to how important it was to them. The most important received a 5, the least important received a 1. The figures shown in Exhibit IV-3 are the average rankings. Except for the commuters who plan to move to New York City,

EXHIBIT IV-3

Railroad Commuters Leisure Time

Characteristic	All Railroad Commuters	Children in Household		Age of Head of Household		State of Residence			Plans to Move to New York		Would Like to Live in a Converted Building[1]	
	$n = 678$	None $n = 214$	Some $n = 457$	<40 yrs. $n = 253$	≥40 yrs. $n = 416$	New York $n = 428$	New Jersey $n = 168$	Connecticut $n = 82$	Yes $n = 70$	No $n = 595$	Yes $n = 74$	No $n = 344$
Times per year commuter comes to New York City for some leisure time activity	11.9	15.9	10.0	13.1	11.3	12.9	9.2	12.9	23.2	10.6	20.1	11.4
Times per month commuter goes out in the suburbs	3.2	3.6	3.0	3.1	3.3	3.0	3.7	3.0	3.4	3.2	3.4	3.3
Ranking of Activities[2]												
Outdoor Recreation	3.6	Same as Universe[3]		3.7	3.5	Same as Universe			3.6	3.6	Same as Universe	
Relaxing at Home	3.4			3.4	3.4				2.9	3.5		
Going out to Eat	3.1			3.1	3.1				3.1	3.1		
Going to movies or plays	2.8			2.9	2.8				2.8	2.8		
Going to museums	2.1			1.9	2.2				2.1	2.1		

Notes: [1]This column reports the responses given by people who have heard of converted buildings (62.2 percent of the commuters).

[2]The respondents were asked to rank the five activities according to how important each was to them. The most important activity was given the rank of 5, and the least important assigned a rank of 1.

[3]"Same as Universe" means that the responses among the various subgroups are not significantly different from each other, and the response shown in the column titled "All Railroad Commuters" is the appropriate figure.

Source: CUPR Survey of Commuters who travel to New York City by railroad, March 1978.

the order of ranking of activities was the same irrespective of differences in there being children in the household, in the age of the head of household, in state of residence, or in liking to live in a converted building. Although the average rankings varied in some cases, the order of importance is: outdoor recreation is most important, followed by relaxing at home, going out to eat, going to movies or plays, and least important is going to museums. The only difference in this order is reported by people who plan to move to New York City, and even here the only difference is that going out to eat is slightly more important than relaxing at home.

When the typical commuter wants to spend some leisure time away from home, he goes to New York City about once a month and to some suburban area about three times a month. His favorite activities are outdoor recreation and relaxing at home. Less favorite are going out to eat, seeing a movie or play, or visiting a museum. People who plan to move to New York and those who would like to live in a converted building differ from this pattern most noticeably in the number of times they go to New York City - nearly twice the frequency characteristic of other commuters.

Subgroups of Commuters: Attitudes Toward New York City

The commuters were asked several questions designed to get a sense of their attitudes toward New York City. Once again the responses these suburbanites give do not yield much variation when several partitions are made (see Exhibit IV-4). For example, the proportion of respondents who say that they would like to live in New York City (22.3 percent) is essentially constant among commuters with and without children, older or younger than 40 years of age, and among those living in New York, New Jersey, and Connecticut. However, more than triple this proportion is to be found among commuters who plan to move to New York City and who would like to live in a converted building. It must be noted here as an interesting aside that of those people who plan to move to New York City, scarcely more than three-quarters of them say they would like to live there. This apparent contradiction could be a function of the plans' being in the future and being based on children's growing up. That is, the commuter

EXHIBIT IV-4

RAILROAD COMMUTERS' ATTITUDES TOWARD NEW YORK CITY

Characteristic	All Railroad Commuters	Children in Household		Age of Head of Household		State of Residence			Plans to Move to New York		Would Like to Live in a Converted Building[1]	
	n = 678	None n = 214	Some n = 457	<40 yrs. n = 253	≥40 yrs. n = 416	New York n = 428	New Jersey n = 168	Connecticut n = 82	Yes n = 70	No n = 525	Yes n = 74	No n = 344
Percentage of Commuters Who Would Like to Live in New York City	22.3%	Same as Universe[2]		Same as Universe		Same as Universe			77.1%	14.8%	70.4%	16.0%
Percentage of Commuters Who Plan to Move to New York City	10.5%	Same as Universe		Same as Universe		12.4%	5.5%	11.0%	100.0%	-	37.1%	7.9%
In how many years? (n=67)	8.4 yrs.	3.9	10.0	10.7	7.3	8.3	9.2	7.6	-		8.2	9.4
Why? (n=67)												
After children grown it would be desirable	39.7%	Same as Universe		Same as Universe		Same as Universe			-		Same as Universe	
Job related	32.5											
Recreation/culture	7.4											
Choice of Housing (n=67)												
High Rise Apartment	60.3%	Same as Universe		Same as Universe		Same as Universe			-		45.0%	70.8%
Brownstone or Townhouse	24.1										45.0	16.7
Garden Apartment	10.3										5.0	12.5
Converted Apartment	1.7										5.0	-

(continued)

EXHIBIT IV-4 *(continued)*

RAILROAD COMMUTERS' ATTITUDES TOWARD NEW YORK CITY

Characteristic	*All Railroad Commuters*	*Children in Household*		*Age of Head of Household*		*State of Residence*			*Plans to Move to New York*		*Would Like to Live in a Converted Building*[1]	
		None	*Some*	*<40 yrs.*	*≥40 yrs.*	*New York*	*New Jersey*	*Connecticut*	*Yes*	*No*	*Yes*	*No*
	n = 678	*n = 214*	*n = 457*	*n = 253*	*n = 416*	*n = 428*	*n = 168*	*n = 82*	*n = 70*	*n = 525*	*n = 74*	*n = 344*
Percentage of Commuters Who Do Not Plan to Move to New York City	89.5%	Same as Universe		Same as Universe		87.6%	94.5%	89.0%	-	100%	62.9%	92.1%
Why? (n=587)												
Lack of suburban amenities	23.3%	32.1%	19.3%	Same as Universe		Same as Universe				-	20.4%	25.8%
General dislike for New York City	17.0	16.0	17.5								2.0	16.5
City unsuitable for small children	14.8	1.6	21.0								28.6	15.8
New York City is too crowded	11.9	11.8	12.0								10.2	10.6
New York City is too expensive	7.3	8.6	6.8								14.3	4.5
Crime Rate	7.2	9.6	6.0								6.1	6.8
Poor city services	4.4	5.9	3.8								4.1	5.2
What could the city do to make you want to move there? (n = 587)												
Nothing	64.9%	64.6%	65.1%	Same as Universe		Same as Universe				-	37.0%	66.3%
Lower incidence of crime	9.5	9.0	9.8								15.2	10.3
Clean the city	8.8	10.6	7.9								8.7	8.7
Lower Cost of Living (Housing, utilities, taxes)	6.3	7.4	5.6								10.9	4.4
Improve schools	3.5	0.5	5.0								13.0	3.3

(continued)

EXHIBIT IV-4 *(continued)*

RAILROAD COMMUTERS' ATTITUDES TOWARD NEW YORK CITY

Characteristic	All Railroad Commuters n = 678	Children in Household		Age of Head of Household		State of Residence			Plans to Move to New York		Would Like to Live in a Converted Building[1]	
		None n = 214	Some n = 457	<40 yrs. n = 253	≥40 yrs. n = 416	New York n = 428	New Jersey n = 168	Connecticut n = 82	Yes n = 70	No n = 525	Yes n = 74	No n = 344
Most Enjoyable Aspect of New York City												
Culture	37.0%	Same as Universe		31.7%	40.4%	Same as Universe			34.3%	37.5%	28.8%	39.6%
Activity, Ambience	23.1			22.1	23.6				38.6	21.2	37.0	24.3
Recreation, Fun, Entertainment	18.4			23.3	15.8				18.6	18.3	19.2	16.4
Nothing	6.3			4.0	7.5				-	7.2	-	6.2
Most Disliked Aspect of New York City												
Filth, pollution	27.4%	Same as Universe		Same as Universe		Same as Universe			22.4%	28.1%	Same as Universe	
Crime	25.3								32.8	24.5		
Crowding, Congestion	21.6								11.9	22.7		
Assuming the Railroad Commuter Had to Move to New York City next year												
Preferred Borough:												
Manhattan	67.9%	73.9%	64.9%	Same as Universe		65.5%	65.5%	83.3%	84.3%	64.7%	87.0%	68.3%
Queens	16.8	16.7	16.8			19.3	13.8	9.7	5.7	18.8	4.3	18.0
Staten Island	8.2	5.9	9.4			7.3	13.8	2.8	5.7	8.8	4.3	7.5
Brooklyn	5.5	3.4	6.5			6.1	4.8	2.8	4.3	5.7	4.3	4.3
Bronx	1.6	-	2.4			1.7	2.1	1.4	-	2.0	-	1.9

(continued)

EXHIBIT IV-4 *(continued)*

RAILROAD COMMUTERS' ATTITUDES TOWARD NEW YORK CITY

Characteristic	*All Railroad Commuters*	*Children in Household*		*Age of Head of Household*		*State of Residence*			*Plans to Move to New York*		*Would Like to Live in a Converted Building*[1]	
	n = 678	*None* *n = 214*	*Some* *n = 457*	*<40 yrs.* *n = 253*	*≥40 yrs.* *n = 416*	*New York* *n = 428*	*New Jersey* *n = 168*	*Connecticut* *n = 82*	*Yes* *n = 70*	*No* *n = 525*	*Yes* *n = 74*	*No* *n = 344*
Assuming the Railroad Commuter Had to Move to New York City next year												
Preferred type of housing:												
High Rise Apartment	31.8%	31.8%	31.7%	23.8%	36.5%	Same as Universe			59.0%	29.0%	35.3%	34.8%
Brownstone/Townhouse	28.7	27.2	29.5	36.9	23.6				21.3	28.5	48.6	28.3
Detached House	28.3	22.1	31.1	33.2	25.9				8.2	31.3	4.4	27.1
Garden Apartment	9.2	16.9	5.7	4.5	11.7				4.9	9.6	1.5	8.2
Converted Building	1.4	2.1	1.1	0.8	1.8				3.3	1.2	8.8	0.9
Monthly rent the commuter would expect to pay:	$479	$441	$498	$497	$460	$458	$486	$578	$601	$462	$538	$511
If rent (property taxes, if owned) and utilities were to double next year, what would you do?												
Remain in current residence	56.7%	Same as Universe		Same as Universe		Same as Universe			64.1%	55.9%	Same as Universe	
Move to another New York City Suburb	13.6								10.9	13.7		
Move to different are entirely	12.5								7.8	1.9		
Move to New York City	2.5								4.7	13.7		

Notes: [1]This column reports the responses given by people who have heard of converted buildings (62.2 percent of the commuters).
[2]"Same as Universe" means that the responses among the various subgroups are not significantly different from each other, and the response shown in the column titled "All Railroad Commuters" is the appropriate figure.

Source: CUPR Survey of Commuters who travel to New York City by railroad, March 1978.

plans to move after his offspring have gong to college, but he would not like to live in New York City until then.

Those who plan to move to the city comprise 10.5 percent of the railroad commuters. The proportion is slightly higher among New York State and Connecticut residents, and nearly twice the percentage of New Jersey commuters. Of the people who said they would like to live in a converted building, nearly four out of ten have plans to move to New York City.

The commuters who plan to move to New York City were asked when and why they planned to move, and what type of residence they would choose. The planned move was relatively far in the future for most of these commuters - 8.4 years. People without children have plans to move sooner, in about four years, most likely as a function of their not being (or no longer being) concerned about schools or other matters associated with rearing a family. The reasons for wanting to move to the city are uniform for all groups of commuters. The predominant explanation is that living in New York City will be more attractive than living in the suburbs after children grow up. And finally, the majority of these commuters intend to live in a high rise apartment, although a substantial proportion desires a brownstone or townhouse. Only 2 percent of these people who plan to move to New York City intend to live in a converted building. Once again these preferences do not vary among the several partitions of respondents, except among those who have answered that they would like to live in a converted building. There is a provocative point to be made about the type of housing chosen by people who say that they would like to live in a converted building. Very few of them gave this as their first choice - only 5 percent. This underscores the point made earlier, that although people say they would like to live in one of these new types of housing, it is not really a competitor with other types of dwellings. It could be that they would only consider recycled units were they unable to find a more traditional residence.

The commuters who do not plan to move to New York City were queried about why they have no such plans, and also about what the city could do that would make them want to move there. Their responses to both questions vary only with the presence or absence of children, and with their saying they would or would not like to live in a converted building. For all commuters, even those in the two partitions that show some variation in the pattern of responses, the principal reasons imply a comparison between New York City and its suburbs in which the city comes up short. The primary reasons are the lack of suburban amenities, a general dislike of the city, and a perception of the city's being unsuitable for rearing children. Similarly, there are few variations in the responses to the question in which commuters were asked if there were anything the city could do to attract them to living there. The large majority of all commuters (except those who would like to live in a converted building) cannot imagine anything that would induce them to live in the city. The people who would like to live in a recycled building are somewhat more hopeful. A substantially greater proportion of these commuters than those uninterested in converted buildings say that a lower incidence of crime, a cleaner city, cheaper housing, or improved schools would draw them to New York City.

The previous two paragraphs have discussed responses made by people who do and do not plan to move to New York City, because each group was asked a different sequence of questions about their reasons for having or not having such an intention. The remainder of the responses to be discussed are replies to questions asked of all the commuters.

The reports about what was the most enjoyable aspect of New York City varied with the age of the commuter, and by whether or not he would like to live in a converted building. Older commuters, those with no plans to move to the city, and those who would not enjoy living in a converted building were most likely to mention that they enjoyed cultural activities in the city. Younger people were more likely to mention recreation, fun, or excitement; and people planning to move to the city or who would like to live in a recycled structure were most likely to mention the ambience of the city.

The most disliked aspect has a more constant distribution of answers among the subgroups of commuters. Filth and other pollution, crime, and crowding or congestion are reported almost equally by most commuters. However, commuters who plan to move to the city are much less bothered by crowding than those without plans to move there.

All commuters were asked to consider the hypothetical situation that they would have to move to New

York City in the next year; they were then asked which borough and type of housing they would prefer under these circumstances, and also how much rent they would expect to have to pay. In every instance, Manhattan was the most preferred borough and Staten Island was least preferred. Households without children were more attracted to Manhattan than those with youngsters; people living in Connecticut were the most attracted to Manhattan; Staten Island was chosen most often by people from New Jersey, although it was rarely chosen at all. Finally, Manhattan was preferred by the greatest proportions of people who plan to move to the city or who would like to live in a converted building. Even with the variations discussed, however, the large majority of commuters in general as well as those in the specific subgroups prefer Manhattan.

There is no clearly preferred type of housing, with nearly equivalent proportions of commuters mentioning high-rise apartments, brownstones or townhouses, and detached houses. Once again there are significant variations in the preferences of the subgroups. The most noteworthy are that a clear majority of the people who plan to move to the city would prefer a high-rise apartment, and that almost half the people who would enjoy living in a converted building report that they would live in a brownstone or townhouse if they had to move to New York City next year. Apparently, being able to imagine that living in a recycled building would be enjoyable does not mean that it would be the first choice for most people.

The monthly rent figure that the commuters would envision having to pay varies in the way that income varies, a pattern discussed earlier. For example, people who live in Connecticut think they would have to pay more than do the residents of New York and New Jersey.

Finally, the commuters were asked what they would do if their housing costs doubled in the next year. The clear majority would stay in their current residence, while less than 3 percent would move to New York City. The only group that shows any variation from the pattern of responses given by all commuters are the people who plan to move to New York City. These people are the <u>most</u> likely to stay in their current residence if the cost of living there doubles, once again indicating how far in the future their plans are. Their intention to move to the city does not seem to be predicated on an intense desire to be there, a desire born from a mass of dissatisfactions with the suburbs; it is a calmer desire, one not very apt to be inflamed even by the instance of greatly increased suburban costs of living.

Subgroups of Commuters: Summary

The characteristics, activities, and attitudes of all commuters have been analyzed in the preceding sections according to several subgroups that they can be divided into. In general, there is little variation among the subgroups with regard to their personal characteristics and their housing characteristics. Commuters who live in Connecticut earn more and live in more expensive houses than their counterparts in New Jersey and New York. People who intend to move to the city earn substantially more money (and live in more expensive houses) than those without such plans. But these are just about the only important distinctions among the personal characteristics of commuters, a finding in some ways disappointing because it precludes the drawing of distinct profiles of commuters who want to move to New York City and of those who would like to live in a converted building.

Similarly, the attitudes toward New York City are remarkably similar for commuters partitioned according to their age, to their having or not having children, to the state where they live, or even according to whether or not they plan to move to the city. The principal distinguishing characteristics of people who plan to move to New York City are their frequent trips to the city for leisure time pursuits.

SUMMARY

Among this group of railroad commuters there is little evidence of a strong desire to move to New York City. For the few who do have plans to move there, the preferred housing is an apartment in a high-rise building. Although converted buildings may have some fashionable appeal at the moment, their charms are not very strongly felt by the commuters. Very few of these suburbanites both say that they are interested in converted units and also mention them as the first choice among housing options in the city. The concept is relatively new, and its popularization is barely nascent.

As yet, judging from the demographic characteristics of people occupying converted buildings, it is a housing option which appeals to people more youthful and less settled than the railroad commuters are (see Chapter 1). Listed below are the principal findings of the survey of commuters.

1. The median age of the commuters is 43.8 years. Typically, the commuter is very well educated (75 percent have at least finished college), works in a highly-skilled occupation (72 percent have white collar jobs), and is very well paid (median annual household income is $36,046).

2. Over half the commuters have lived in New York City. Their reasons for having moved out of the city are that they wanted to own a house (27 percent), wanted to enjoy suburban amenities (27 percent), or wanted to live in an environment more suitable for children than the city (19 percent).

3. Although the average commuting time is two and a half hours each day, the respondents are very well contented. When asked to rate satisfaction, using a scale from 1 to 5 on which 5 is very satisfied, the average rating was 4.2. The satisfaction is also apparent in the commuters' intentions to remain in their residence an average of 12 years.

4. Outdoor recreation and relaxing at home are the most favored leisure time activities of these suburbanites. Going out to eat and going to movies or plays follow, and least important is going to museums.

5. On the average, the commuters go to New York City once a month for some kind of entertainment.

6. Eleven percent of the commuters intend to move to New York City, but these plans are about 8 years in the future. Only 13 percent of them know of and would like to live in a converted building.

7. Asked to consider the hypothetical situation that they would have to move to New York City in the next year, the commuters were queried about which borough they would prefer, the kind of housing they would seek, and how much they would expect to have to pay for it. The overwhelming choice was an apartment or brownstone in Manhattan, and the typical respondent expected to pay approximately 12 percent more for a place in the city than for his current residence.

8. Commuters find New York City most enjoyable for the cultural activities there, for the excitement or ambience of the city, and for the entertainment to be found. Interestingly, the pattern of responses does not vary according to how the commuters have ranked the importance of leisure time activities. For example, people for whom going to museums is not very important do not mention the enjoyment of these cultural activities any less often than people who rate going to museums as most important. A possible explanation is that for many commuters it is important that in the city there be cultural activities, regardless of the commuter's use of these activities.

9. The most disliked aspects of New York City are filth and pollution (27 percent), crime (25 percent), and crowding or congestion (22 percent).

10. When asked what they would do if their monthly housing costs were to double, 57 percent said they would pay the increase. Only 3 percent would move to New York City.

11. The intention to move to the city that 11 percent of the commuters report does not seem to be predicated on an intense desire to be there, a desire born from a mass of dissatisfactions with the suburbs. It is a calmer desire, one not very apt to be inflamed even by the instance of greatly increased suburban costs of housing.

12. The most important distinguishing characteristics between commuters who do and do not plan to move to New York City are their incomes and

the frequency with which they come to the city for entertainment. Suburbanites who intend to move to the city have median household incomes of $48,013, nearly 40 percent higher than the median reported by those with no such intentions ($34,841 per year). And the commuters who plan a move to the city come there twice as often for entertainment than do the suburbanites without plans to move.

13. The personal characteristics and the attitudes toward New York, summarized above for all the railroad commuters, are virtually invariant when all these respondents are partitioned according to their age, to their having or not having children, to the state in which they live, and even according to whether or not they plan to move to the city. They are, in short, a very homogeneous group with respect to the questions that this study asked.

FOOTNOTES

1. S. Gregory Lipton, "Evidence of Central City Revival," Journal of the American Institute of Planners (Volume 43: April, 1977), p. 146.

2. Harold S. Jensen, "The Future of Cities," Urban Land (Volume 37: February 1978), p. 3.

3. Tri-State Regional Planning Commission, Interim Technical Report 4549-1302.

4. Ibid.

Chapter 5

THE FISCAL IMPACT OF THE J-51 PROGRAM TO ENCOURAGE RESIDENTIAL CONVERSIONS

INTRODUCTION

It was noted in Chapter 2 that several studies have concluded that the benefits of the Section 421 program will more than pay for the revenues lost from the program's tax breaks. This chapter will analyze the effect of the J-51 tax benefits so that a conclusion can be made about the cost of encouraging conversions in New York City.

Several rationales for offering tax benefits to encourage conversion of commercial and industrial buildings to residential use were discussed in Chapter 1. Briefly, these were improved neighborhoods, decreased vacancies and tax delinquencies among existing structures, better maintained buildings, and an increased housing supply. Chapter 1 described the people who have been attracted to living in converted units, making clear that these are people very interested in staying in the city, people employed in highly skilled jobs, and people with enough money to spend on the felicities and necessities of life that their presence in neighborhoods will attract services to those areas, and this means business and jobs.

Although the benefits of encouraging conversions may be sufficient to convince the city to extend J-51 incentives, and although the city does not have to raise money to pay for the conversions, there is a cost attendant to the program that must be quantified. The J-51 program costs New York City money in foregone tax revenues and in the extension of municipal services into previously non-residential areas, but it also creates money for the city through construction expenditures, from sales and income taxes collected, and in the prospect of the property taxes that will be collected after the J-51 benefits to a specific building have been exhaust This chapter will sum the explicit revenues and the costs and thereby determine the fiscal impact on the city generated by a unit converted under the J-51 program.

The analysis which follows quantifies the costs and revenues that are directly related to conversions that occur because of the J-51 tax benefits program. There are, of course, many other less direct effects, but these are nearly impossible to quantify. When a building is converted successfully, the resulting increased residential activity and the services which open to accommoda the tenants can cause a dramatic rise in property values (and thereby in city tax receipts) of buildings adjacent to the converted one. It may be possible to measure this by looking at turnover rates of buildings proximate to converted structures, but some portion of any increased sales activity would have taken place, albeit elsewhere in New York City, had there been no conversion. Similarly, individual decisions by shopkeepers and by taxpaying residents to leave the city may have been reconsidered because of the new vitality manifest in conversions of partially vacant buildings, but these changes in plans would be extremely difficult to identify This brief discussion implies that the fiscal impact of encouraging conversions by tax benefits is very elusive when indirect effects are considered. It does mean, however, that the results of the analysis which follows are conservative, that they understate the benefits that will be enjoyed by the city because of encouraging conversions. Throughout the analysis will be found comments that indicate the source and likely magnitude of indirect, unquantified effects.

QUANTIFYING THE COSTS AND REVENUES

Fundamental to the analysis which follows are several assumptions:

1. The tax rate on assessed valuation of real property will remain a constant 9 percent.

2. The economic life span of a project is 25 years. This means that all costs and revenues which accrue are extended for 25 years, then discounted to the current year.

3. The discount rate is set at 8 percent. Although this assumes some moderation of the city's current money costs, it is a rate that is somewhat higher than the rate has been in the past.

4. Many of the items to be considered will vary depending on the relationship between the dwelling units under consideration and the potential residence/work place of their occupants. If a resident would have moved to the suburbs had a converted unit not been avilable, he will be termed an induced resident. An induced resident pays sales and income taxes, and spends money in the city, which would have been lost if a converted unit had not been available. These revenues can be said to serve as an offset to the cost to the city of the J-51 program.

   If the resident would have lived in the city whether or not the converted unit had been available, he would have paid sales and income taxes and spent money in the city irrespective of the type of unit, and thus creates no offsetting revenues to subtract from the cost of the J-51 incentives.

Using these assumptions, it is possible to identify eight categories of costs and revenues attendant both to the benefits of the J-51 program and to the residents who are induced to live in the city because of a unit converted under the provisions of this abatement and exemption program. The detailed calculations which will be presented yield eight primary costs or revenues for each converted unit:

1. Real estate taxes foregone or created due to the exemption and abatement provisions of the J-51 program for each unit.

2. Tax revenues produced by construction spending for each converted unit.

3. Tax revenues collected because of multiplier effects of construction spending for each converted unit.

4. Sales and income taxes paid by a resident induced to stay in New York City.

5. Tax revenues generated by net spending of induced residents.

6. Real property taxes collected because of expanded commercial space due to spending by induced residents.

7. Per capita cost for the provision of common municipal services for induced residents.

8. Other New York City tax revenues and fees.

The next eight sections will specify the calculations used to determine these total costs and revenues. The methodology used is based on that developed by George Sternlieb, Elizabeth Roistacher, and James Hughes in Tax Subsidies and Housing Investment, published by the Center for Urban Policy Research.

Real Estate Taxes Foregone or Created by the J-51 Program

Under amendments signed by Mayor Beame on December 30, 1975, the city's program for encouraging rehabilitation through tax abatement and exemption was expanded to give benefits to nonresidential buildings that were converted to apartments. Section J-51 - 2.5 of the Administrative Code of the City of New York contains four provisions used to determine the amount of abatement and exemption allowed a landlord for the conversion of commercial property to residential use. First, there is a 12-year exemption from any increase in taxes resulting from improvements to the property. In effect, the assessed valuation of the property remains constant for twelve years. Second, the Department of Development reviews the landlord's list of improvements and their costs, and calculates a reasonable cost of conversion. A total of 90 percent of this reasonable cost may be deducted from real estate levies as an abatement. The maximum annual abatement is now limited to 8.33 percent of the reasonable cost of conversion that was determined by the Department of Development. The abatement cannot exceed the current levy on the property, i.e., the city cannot owe the landlord money. Finally, the full abatement must be written off in not less than nine nor more than 20 years.

In October, 1977, the Real Estate Board of New York, Inc., released a report entitled "Review of the First Year's Experience Under the New J-51 Program," which studied the costs of all the commercial conversions that received J-51 benefits. The per unit figures that appeared in the study are the basis for all calculations in this chapter. The average assessed valuation before improvements was $6321 per unit; after improvements it was $13,096. Landlords reported spending $15,246 per unit on improvements, of which $10,672 was certified as reasonable costs.

The yearly taxes created by the J-51 program, shown in Exhibit V-1 to start in the fifteenth year, are the total assessed value of the converted unit times the tax rate. The taxes based on the assessment before conversion have not been subtracted from the total tax bill in order to account for the confluent effect of two factors. First, there are significant delinquencies among commercial buildings, and if units were not converted, the delinquency rate could well increase for the reasons discussed in Chapter 1. Second, after the twelfth year of the J-51 benefits, a converted building will not be protected against increased assessment. In the neighborhoods where conversions are occurring, the increased liveliness and attractiveness of the area could cause the market and assessed value of property to rise dramatically. Thus, the decision to term all the taxes collected from a converted unit "taxes created" is, in our opinion, a conservative statement of the effects the J-51 program will have on delinquency rates and property values.

Using these figures and assuming that the economic life span of a converted unit is 25 years, that the tax rate will remain constant at 9 percent, and that the proper discount rate is 8 percent, *Exhibit V-1*

EXHIBIT V-1

COST/REVENUE CALCULATIONS
J-51 COST/UNIT
(Constant Tax Rate)

Year	Initial Assessment[1]	Certified Reasonable Cost[1]	Converted Assessment[1]	Exempted Portion of Assessment[2]	Tax Rate	Tax that is Exempted[3]	Tax[4]	Abatement[5]	Yearly Total Tax Foregone[6]	$\frac{1}{(1.08)^t}$	Discounted Present Value of Taxes Foregone[7]	Yearly Taxes Created[8]	Discounted Present Value of Taxes Created[8]
0	6,321	10,672	13,096	6775	.0900	$610	$569	$569	$1179	1.0000	$1179		
1				6775	.0900	610	569	569	1179	.9259	1092		
2				6775	.0900	610	569	569	1179	.8573	1011		
3				6775	.0900	610	569	569	1179	.7938	936		
4				6775	.0900	610	569	569	1179	.7350	867		
5				6775	.0900	610	569	569	1179	.6806	802		
6				6775	.0900	610	569	569	1179	.6302	743		
7				6775	.0900	610	569	569	1179	.5835	688		
8				6775	.0900	610	569	569	1179	.5403	637		
9				6775	.0900	610	569	569	1179	.5002	590		
10				6775	.0900	610	569	569	1179	.4632	546		
11				6775	.0900	610	569	569	1179	.4289	506		
12					.0900		1179	1179	1179	.3971	468		
13					.0900		1179	1179	1179	.3677	434		
14					.0900		1179	419	419	.3405	401	760	259
15					.0900		1179			.3152	Σ=$10,900	1179	372
16					.0900		1179			.2919		1179	344
17					.0900		1179			.2703		1179	319
18					.0900		1179			.2503		1179	295
19					.0900		1179			.2317		1179	273
20					.0900		1179			.2145		1179	253
21					.0900		1179			.1986		1179	234
22					.0900		1179			.1839		1179	217
23					.0900		1179			.1702		1179	201
24					.0900		1179			.1577		1179	186
													Σ=$2,953

NET LOSS OVER LIFE OF PROJECT = $7947, discounted present value.

(continued)

EXHIBIT V-1 *(continued)*

COST/REVENUE CALCULATIONS
J-51 COST/UNIT
(Constant Tax Rate)

Notes: [1]The figures for initial assessment, certified reasonable cost, and converted assessment are based on averages found in "Review of the First Year's Experience Under the New J-51 Program" prepared by the Real Estate Board of New York, Inc.

[2]This figure is the difference between the Converted Assessment and the Initial Assessment.

[3]The exempted tax is the product of the tax rate and the exempted portion of the assessment.

[4]The figure shown in this column is the product of the tax rate and the converted assessment less the exempted portion of that assessment, i.e., it is the tax rate times the initial assessment.

[5]The J-51 program allows for the yearly assessed tax to be abated to a total of no more than 90 percent of the certified reasonable cost. The full specifications of the J-51 section of the Administrative Code can be found in the text.

[6]This is the total of assessed tax that is exempted and abated.

[7]This is the product of the present value calculation times the total yearly tax foregone.

[8]This is the tax that will be collected once the J-51 benefits have been exhausted.

[9]This is the product of the present value calculations times the yearly taxes created.

shows that the city will incur a loss of $7,947, discounted present value, in taxes foregone over the lifetime of each converted unit before offsets.

Tax Revenues Produced by Construction Spending[1]

The report by the Real Estate Research Board cited earlier found that landlords spent $15,246 to improve each converted unit. This spending not only represents new jobs and more business in the city, it also implies direct tax revenues through taxation of the initial round of spending and through taxation of additional spending that occurs via multiplier effects.[2] The latter taxation will be quantified in the next section. Assuming that half of the labor used for conversions are city residents, that because of the high sales tax in the city only one-third of the material is purchased there, and that 35 percent of owners' spending on conversions is for materials and 65 percent is for labor,[3] *the total tax revenues produced by the initial spending on construction for each unit is equal to $237 (see Exhibit V-2).*

Tax Revenues Created Through Multiplier Effects of Construction Spending[4]

If a unit cost $15,246 to convert to residential use, and if a local multiplier of 1.67 (comparable to a conservative 0.4 marginal propensity to consume locally)[5] is assumed, then the induced income generation of the initial spending is equal to $10,215. It is estimated that approximately 8 percent of local spending returns to the city as tax revenue through sales, income, and property taxation.[6] (It is this taxation itself that limits the multiplier effect because taxes are one form of leakage from the spending stream.) Hence, induced spending effects eventually generate $817 in tax revenues. Since it takes some time for these effects to occur, the $817 should be divided over a three-year period, then discounted back to present value using the assumed rate of 8 percent. *As Exhibit V-3 shows, the result is a contribution of $757 to the total cost of any unit that would not otherwise have been converted.*

EXHIBIT V-2

Estimated Tax Revenues Generated Directly from Induced Construction Spending

Conversion Costs per unit: $15,246

Labor Costs: .65 x $15,246 = $9,910

Labor Income to City Residents:
.5 x $9910 = $4,955

Income Taxes[1]/Paid on Labor Income by City Residents: .015 x $4955 =	*$74*

Labor Income to Non-city Residents:
.5 x $9910 = $4,955

Income Taxes[2]/Paid on Labor Income by Non-Residents: .0045 x $4955 =	*$22*

Cost of Materials: .35 x $15,246 = $5,336

Materials Purchased in New York City:
.33 x $5,336 = $1,761

City Sales Taxes on Purchased Materials = .08 x $1,761 =	*$141*
TOTAL TAXES ACCRUING TO THE CITY FROM CONSTRUCTION SPENDING:	*$237*

Notes: [1]Estimated average tax rate on before-tax income; Office of Management and Budget, The City of New York.

[2]Actual nonresident income tax rates; Office of Management and Budget, The City of New York.

EXHIBIT V-3

DETERMINATION OF PRESENT VALUE OF TAX REVENUES DERIVED FROM MULTIPLIER EFFECTS OF CONSTRUCTION COST

$$\text{Present Value} = \sum_{t=o}^{2} 272 \left(\frac{1}{1.08}\right)^t$$

t	Tax Revenues	$\left(\frac{1}{1.08}\right)^t$	Present Value
0	$272	1.0000	$272
1	272	.9259	252
2	272	.8573	233
	TOTAL PRESENT VALUE:		$757

Sales and Income Taxes Created by Induced Residents

The interviews with people living in converted buildings show that their median income is $21,783, and that the average household size is roughly two people. These elements of information are the basis of the calculation of sales and income tax for a typical household induced to stay in New York City by a residence in a converted building. The yearly budget of this typical household, which appears in Exhibit V-4, is compiled by calculating the federal, state, and city tax levies for two persons filing jointly and claiming standard deductions. The average rent and utility bill paid for units in converted buildings are taken from the interviews with residents, and are $393 per month for rent and $38 for utilities. Expenditures on food at and away from home are based on data in the "1972 Diary Data" from the Consumer Expenditure Survey Series of the United States Bureau of Labor Statistics. The diary data on both types of food expenditures for a household of two people with an income between $20,000 and $24,999 is adjusted to account for the family's living in a Northeastern SMSA. Finally, the adjusted food expenditures are inflated according to the increases in the New York City SMSA Consumer Price Index from 1972 to November, 1977 (the most recent edition of the index). Exhibit V-5 reproduces the expenditures determined by these adjustments. The telephone expense is an estimate. All other items are approximated using the "Autumn 1976 Urban Worker Family of Four of New York-Northeastern New Jersey (Intermediate Budget)" prepared by the Bureau of Labor Statistics, with some adjustments made to account for a two-person household.

It is assumed that even if the household induced to live in the city had not been so induced, the workers would still have been employed in New York City. Therefore, the net injection of income taxes is equal to the difference between resident income taxes and nonresident taxes. Resident income taxes are calculated to be $432, while the nonresidential taxes would be $94. Therefore, the total additional income taxes collected from an induced household is equal to $338 (see Exhibit V-6).[7]

Net collections of sales taxes from an induced household are computed on the items subject to sales tax included in the family budget shown in Exhibit V-4. These base figures are adjusted to account for expenditures made outside the city and for expenditures that

EXHIBIT V-4

ESTIMATED ANNUAL HOUSEHOLD BUDGET, TWO-PERSON HOUSEHOLD IN CONVERTED BUILDING TOTAL INCOME OF $21,783

	Dollars	*Percentage of Total*
Income Taxes[1]		
Federal	$3381	15.5%
State	1223	5.6
City	432	2.0
Rent[2]	4716	21.6
*Utilities[2]	456	2.1
*Telephone[3]	218	1.0
Food at Home[4]	2281	10.5
*Food Away from Home[4]	1796	8.2
*Clothing and Personal Care[5]	1289	5.9
Medical Care[5]	859	3.9
Transportation[5,6]	1198	5.5
*Miscellaneous Taxable[5]	1566	7.2
Miscellaneous Non-taxable[7]	1145	5.3
Savings[7]	1223	5.6
TOTAL	$21,783	100.0

Notes: [1]Taxes are calculated assuming two exemptions and a standard deduction for a couple filing jointly.

[2]Rent and utilities payments are the averages reported during CUPR interviews with residents living in converted buildings. These interviews were conducted during August and September, 1977.

[3]Only $164 of the phone bill is subject to City taxes.

[4]Food at home and food away from home are based on data from the Consumer Expenditure Survey Series, Diary Data 1972, "Selected Weekly Expenditures Cross-Classified by Family Characteristics." The food categories for a two-person household with a before-tax income between $20,000 and $24,999 for all U.S. families is adjusted according to food expenditure data

NOTES TO EXHIBIT V-4 (continued)

for families in SMSAs in the Northeastern United States. This data is from the same series of reports. Finally, the adjusted expenditures are increased according to changes in the consumer price index for the cost of living in New York City from 1972 to 1977. The calculations are approximate (see Exhibit V-5).

[5]Estimation of expenditures for clothing and personal care, medical care, transportation, and miscellaneous taxable and non-taxable items is based on data from the intermediate level Urban Worker Family Budget for New York-Northeastern New Jersey - Autumn 1976, U.S. Department of Labor, Bureau of Labor Statistics, Middle Atlantic Region, "Selected Weekly Expenditures Cross-Classified by Family Characteristics." The food categories for a two-person household with a before-tax income between $20,000 and $24,999 for all U.S. families is adjusted according to food expenditure data for families in SMSAs in the Northeastern United States. This data is from the same series of reports. Finally, the adjusted expenditures are increased according to changes in the consumer price index for the cost of living in New York City from 1972 to 1977. The calculations are approximate (see Exhibit V-5).

[6]It is assumed that the household owns an automobile which is not garaged, and that it makes outlays for gasoline, maintenance, and auto insurance, as well as for public transportation.

[7]This includes social security, insurance, and charitable contributions.

*Subject to 4 percent city sales tax. These items are the basis for calculation of city sales tax revenues shown in Exhibit V-6.

EXHIBIT V-5

ESTIMATED EXPENDITURES FOR FOOD AT HOME AND FOOD AWAY FROM HOME

	Weekly Expenditures on Food, Family of Two, Before-Tax Income of $20,000-$24,999		
	U.S. Rural and Urban[1]	*Adjusted to Northeast (Inside SMSA's)*[2]	*Adjusted to to Nov., 1977*[3]
Food at Home	$21.38	$24.46	$43.86
Food Away from Home	16.03	19.25	34.53

Notes: [1]Consumer Expenditure Survey Survey Series: Diary Data 1972, U.S. Department of Labor, Bureau of Labor Statistics, Report 448-1, Table 2. Data collected for the period July 1972-June 1973.

[2]Using data from Table 15 of Report 448-1 citied above, it was found that for all family sizes and incomes, expenditures for food at home for families living inside SMSAs in the Northeast were 14.4 percent higher than for all U.S. families. This fact was used to increase the weekly expenditure reported for expenditures for food at home. Similarly, families in SMSAs in the Northeast spend 20.1 percent more for food away form home than do all families in the United States. This percentage was used to increment the weekly figure shown in the first column of figures.

[3]Between July, 1972, and November 1977, the Consumer Price Index for the New York Metropolitan region increased from 131.4 to 188.5, a percentage increase of 43.5%. Since food prices are among the most rapidly increasing components of the index, the budgets have been increased by 25 percent above the change shown in the index as a whole. This is intended to take into account both the high rate of increase and a slight reduction in consumption.

EXHIBIT V-6

ESTIMATED FEDERAL, STATE, AND LOCAL INCOME TAXES FOR HOUSEHOLD OF TWO, INCOME OF $21,783, ASSUMING THE STANDARD DEDUCTION AND TWO EXEMPTIONS – 1977

```
Federal Calculation
  From Tax Table B, tax is $3,381      Federal Tax     $3,381

State Calculation
  $21,783 Gross Income
    2,000 Standard Deduction
    1,300 Exemption: 2 x $650

  $18,483 Adjusted Gross Income
          Tax = $1,060 + .11 ($18,483 - $17,000)

              = $1,060 + $163

              = $1,223                 State Tax       $1,223

City Calculation - Residents
  $21,783 Gross Income
    2,000 Standard Deduction
    1,300 Exemption:  2 x $650

  $18,483 Adjusted Gross Income
          Tax = $383 + .033 ($18,483 - $17,000)

              = $383 + $49

              = $432                   Resident City
                                          Tax          $  432

City Calculation - Non-Residents
  $21,783 Gross Income
    1,000 Exclusion

  $20,783 Adjusted Gross Income

          Tax = .0045 x $20,783

          Tax = $94                    Non-Resident
                                          City Tax     $   94
```

---

would have been made in the city even if the household had lived elsewhere. A 15 percent reduction is made in the categories of food away from home and miscellaneous taxable items to account for expenditures outside New York City (most likely to occur during vacations).[8] Only the local portion of the telephone bill is subject to taxation, and here it is asssumed that 75 percent of the telephone usage is local. When these adjustments are made, the total taxable outlay is $5401. The state and city sales tax rate is 8 percent, and so the total outlay can be apportioned to $5001 for purchases plus $400 in state and local sales taxes. The local share of this levy is $200 (a 4 percent city sales tax rate).*

It was noted above that 15 percent of the sales taxes would have been collected by the city if the household had lived elsewhere. Hence, the net collection of sales taxes from a household induced to live in New York City is $170 (see Exhibit V-7).

The total of sales and income taxes collected from a family induced to live in the city is $508 ($338 + $170). If income and expenditures grow at 6 percent per year, the present discounted value of the flow over twenty-five years (assuming that city income taxes and sales taxes remain the same) is equal to $10,243, again using an 8 percent discount rate (see Exhibit V-8).[9]

Tax Revenues Collected Because of Multiplier Effects of Net Spending by Induced Residents

The expenditures made by induced residents within New York City will result in increased revenue to the city because of taxes paid by merchants who are part of the local economy. Using a multiplier of 1.67, based on a local marginal propensity to consume of 0.4, the household's expenditures of approximately $13,697, excluding taxes,[10] would result in an additional $9177 stream of spending. Such spending would allow the city to collect $734 in tax revenues through real estate, sales, and income taxes.[11] Such a stream of revenues would take time to develop, here it will be assumed

---

*Though not detailed here, it is evident that the State of New York receives significant fiscal benefits from the program.

EXHIBIT V-7

ESTIMATED COLLECTION OF SALES TAXES FROM AN INDUCED FAMILY OF TWO, ANNUAL INCOME OF $21,783

Taxable Items [1]			
Utilities	$ 456		
Telephone [2]	164		
Food Away from Home [3]	1527		
Clothing and Personal Care	1289		
Miscellaneous Taxable [3]	1331		
Auto Maintenance (including gas) [4]	634		
TOTAL			$5401
Expenditures Excluding 4 Percent City Sales Tax and 4 percent State Sales Tax	$5401 / 1.08	=	$5001
Portion of Sales Tax Levy collected by the City $5001 x .04 =			$200
Total City Sales Tax Paid Less 15 percent for expenditures which would have been made as a nonresident	$ 200 - 30		
NET COLLECTION OF CITY SALES TAX From an Induced Household			$170

[1]See Exhibit V-4 for total family budget.

[2]Reduced to include only local portion of telephone bill.

[3]Reduced by 15 percent to account for expenditures outside the city.

[4]It is assumed that the household has $337 in auto maintenance expenses (excluding gasoline) which includes 8 percent city and state sales taxes. The remaining $297 is the cost of gasoline net of all taxes except state and city sales taxes. (This assumes a price of 55¢ per gallon net of all taxes and is based on consumption of 500 gallons of gasoline per year, which is assumed to be the local portion of gasoline purchases. This is equivalent to driving 7500 miles at 15 miles per gallon.) These auto expenses are a subset of the transportation allotment shown in Exhibit V-4, which includes car insurance as well as expenditures for public transportation and taxicabs. While taxi fleets pay sales taxes on fares, the taxi outlay made by the household is estimated to be no more than $100, so that city taxes generated would be no more than $4. This amount is small enough to ignore.

EXHIBIT V-8

DETERMINATION OF PRESENT VALUE OF SALES AND INCOME TAXES COLLECTED FROM AN INDUCED HOUSEHOLD

$$\textit{Present Value} = \sum_{t=o}^{2} 272 \left(\frac{1}{1.08}\right)^t$$

t	*Sales and Income Taxes*	$(\frac{1.06}{1.08})^t$	*Present Value*
0	$508	1.0000	$508
1	508	.9815	499
2	508	.9633	489
3	508	.9455	480
4	508	.9280	471
5	508	.9109	463
6	508	.8940	454
7	508	.8775	446
8	508	.8612	437
9	508	.8453	429
10	508	.8297	421
11	508	.8143	414
12	508	.7993	406
13	508	.7845	399
14	508	.7699	391
15	508	.7557	384
16	508	.7417	377
17	508	.7280	370
18	508	.7145	363
19	508	.7013	356
20	508	.6883	350
21	508	.6756	343
22	508	.6631	337
23	508	.6508	331
24	508	.6388	325
	TOTAL PRESENT VALUE:		$10,243

to require two years, so that the present discounted value of such a stream would be somewhat less, or $675. Once started, such a stream would be generated each year, and indeed would increase as incomes increase. Assuming a 6 percent rate of growth of expenditures and an 8 percent discount rate, the present value of the multiplier effects for a 25 year period actually totals $13,610 (see Exhibit V-9).[12]

Generation of Real Property Taxes Through Expansion of Commercial Space Due to Spending by Induced Residents

In addition to the taxes collected due to multiplier effects of induced resident spending, the same spending represents increased sales to individual merchants, which will eventuate in increased commercial space. The increased space means additional revenues to the city from property tax levies. Based on data which quantifies the relationship between sales volumes and rents for various quantities of consumer goods, and assuming that 25 percent of a merchant's rent goes to property taxes, it is possible to calculate the long run effects of induced consumer spending.[13] The rent-sales ratio varies with expenditure category. Exhibit V-10 shows the increase in spending by induced residents for each of several categories, the rent-sales ratio, and the increase in property taxes derived from such spending.[14] Increased property tax payments for telephone and utilities are estimated more directly by applying the ratio of property taxes to total revenues for each of the categories,using the assumption that the firms are in a range of constant long run average costs, in which case marginal costs would be equal to average costs. This is a proper assumption to make about telephone and utilities companies, which are in existence because of scale economies and may well be in the range of exhausting such economies.

Total property taxes generated by expansion of commercial space initiated by induced residents' spending is equal to $165. While it could be argued that expanded commercial space is a long term effect of increased spending, it will be assumed here that property tax assessments will increase with increments in a

EXHIBIT V-9

DETERMINATION OF PRESENT VALUE OF MULTIPLIER EFFECTS OF SPENDING BY INDUCED RESIDENTS

$$\text{Present Value} = \sum_{t=o}^{24} \left(\frac{1.06}{1.08}\right)^t$$

t	*Multiplier Effects of Spending*	$\left(\frac{1.06}{1.08}\right)^t$	*Present Value*
0	$675	1.0000	$675
1	675	.9815	663
2	675	.9633	650
3	675	.9455	638
4	675	.9280	626
5	675	.9109	615
6	675	.8940	603
7	675	.8775	592
8	675	.8612	581
9	675	.8453	571
10	675	.8297	560
11	675	.8143	550
12	675	.7993	540
13	675	.7845	530
14	675	.7699	520
15	675	.7557	510
16	675	.7417	501
17	675	.7280	491
18	675	.7145	482
19	675	.7013	473
20	675	.6883	465
21	675	.6756	456
22	675	.6631	448
23	675	.6508	439
24	675	.6388	431
	TOTAL PRESENT VALUE:		$13,610

EXHIBIT V-10

ESTIMATED GENERATION OF REAL PROPERTY TAXES THROUGH EXPANSION OF COMMERCIAL SPACE DUE TO SPENDING BY INDUCED RESIDENTS

Items	*Annual Expenditure of Typical Household* [1]	*Estimated Ratio of Rent to Sales*	*Ratio of Property Taxes to Rent*	*Estimated Increase in Real Property Taxes of Seller*
Utilities[2]	$ 456			$ 46
Telephone[3]	218			17
Food at Home	2,281	.03	.25	17
Food Away from Home[4]	1,527	.08	.25	31
Clothing and Personal Care	1,289	.08	.25	26
Medical Care	859	.05	.25	11
Miscellaneous Taxable[4]	1,331	.05	.25	17
TOTAL:				$165

Notes: [1]Outlays based on a two-person household with an annual income of $21,783. See Exhibit V-4.

[2]Approximately 10 percent of revenues of Consolidated Edison are paid out in real property taxes (Charles Kaiser, "Assessing Real Estate for Taxation at 100 Percent of Full Market Value," New York Times, 10 March, 1976, p. 36).

[3]Approximately 8 percent of revenues of New York Telephone are paid out in real property taxes (New York Telephone Company Annual Report 1974, p. 6).

[4]Reduced by 15 percent from entry in Exhibit V-4 to account for expenditures outside the city.

business' receipts.* This assumption means that the property taxes generated because of expanded commercial activity will start to be collected by the city when the J-51 project is completed. Assuming once again a constant tax rate of 9 percent on assessed valuation and a discount rate of 8 percent, the present value of property taxes from expanded commercial space to meet the needs of induced residents is equal to $1901 (see Exhibit V-11).[15]

Estimating the Per Capita Cost of Common Municipal Services

It is difficult to determine the point at which additional households necessitate expanded city services. Typically, services do not expand with small increments in households, but rather are increased when a substantial number of additional households has accumulated. Graphically this can be described by a step function which shows the level and cost of services to remain constant over a range of numbers of households, then to jump to a higher plateau when some number of additional households has located in the city -- and again to remain constant over a range of numbers of additional households. Such a discrete function can be approximated by smoothly rising curves which represent per capita costs of services. This representation is fairly accurate if the long run average cost curve of municipal services is in the range of minimum long run average costs (which means that all scale economies are being captured), because then the long run marginal cost of services can be approximated by the per capita long run cost. Thus our analysis uses current per capita costs. It may well be argued that given their socio-economic characteristics, the group of conversion tenants conumes less than this amount, however.

Data on budgetary outlays for New York City for Fiscal Year 1977 are used to determine the per capita costs of common municipal services for that year. Exhibit V-12 displays this budget and indicates those expenditures that have been defined as common municipal functions. These items, essentially all those shown

*It should be noted that both conceptually, and in the long run realistically, the result to the city's assessment base is similar even if the new sales merely fortify the basic economics of extant facilities.

EXHIBIT V-11

Determination of Present Value of Real Property Taxes of Expanded Commercial Space

$$Present\ Value = \sum_{t=0}^{24} \left(\frac{1}{1.08}\right)^t$$

t	*Real Property Tax*	$\left(\frac{1}{1.08}\right)^t$	*Present Value*
0	$165	1.0000	$165
1	165	.9259	153
2	165	.8573	141
3	165	.7938	131
4	165	.7350	121
5	165	.6806	112
6	165	.6302	104
7	165	.5835	96
8	165	.5403	89
9	165	.5002	83
10	165	.4632	76
11	165	.4289	71
12	165	.3971	66
13	165	.3677	61
14	165	.3405	56
15	165	.3152	52
16	165	.2919	48
17	165	.2703	45
18	165	.2503	41
19	165	.2317	38
20	165	.2145	35
21	165	.1986	33
22	165	.1839	30
23	165	.1702	28
24	165	.1577	26
	TOTAL PRESENT VALUE:		$1,901

EXHIBIT V-12

NEW YORK CITY EXPENDITURES BY DEPARTMENT GROUPING FISCAL YEAR 1977

Department	
*Legislative	$ 35,835,000
*General Government, City and County	420,195,000
*Libraries	52,779,000
Education	3,258,497,000
*Cultural, etc.	21,563,000
*Municipal Parks	88,914,000
*Public Safety	1,278,318,000
*Sanitation	375,750,000
*Health Services	238,298,000
Hospitals	704,626,000
Social Welfare	3,552,123,000
*Correction	101,143,000
*City Judicial	84,504,000
*County Judicial	6,556,000
*Public Service	30,723,000
Debt Service (including MAC)	1,996,053,000
Human Resources Administration	221,440,000
Model Cities Administration	21,157,000
Judgement and Claims	46,273,000
Transportation	103,000,000
*Miscellaneous	945,564,000
TOTAL	$13,583,311,000
*SUBTOTAL	$ 3,680,142,000

Source: Fiscal Year 1977 expenditures from a telephone conversation with Don Ayalon, Office of Management and Budget, the City of New York.

save hospitals, education, and debt service, total $3.680 billion. The city receives State and Federal aid which partially offsets these expenditures. Exhibit V-13 details the amounts and sources of intergovernmental aid, and shows that the city itself pays $3.244 billion for common services. The city population was estimated as 7.491 million as of 1975. The 1977 average per capita outlay on common municipal services can therefore be approximated as $433. The excluded items either are not used significantly by the new tenantry, as is the case for hospitals and schools, or are relatively constant, as debt service. For example, the cost of new physical facilities is most likely not needed, given the tenantry's demographic and consumption characteristics.

If these costs are expected to grow at 6 percent per year, and if they are discounted at 8 percent per year, then the present discounted per capita cost for the next 25 years is equal to $8730 per person, or $17,460 per household of two (see Exhibit V-14).

Other Revenues and Fees

The city will collect several other classes of revenue from the conversion activity sponsored by the J-51 program. Using data from the report by the Real Estate Board cited earlier, it is found that the city collects $75 per unit for the Real Property Transfer Tax; $116 per unit for the Mortgage Recording Tax; $20 per unit from J-51 application and filing fees; and $48 from Buildings Department fees.[16]

One stipulation of the J-51 Program is that real estate taxes and water changes must be current. This requirement results in revenue to the city both from developers who must pay the arrearages, and from owners who are encouraged to pay the taxes and charges in anticipation of selling their building for residential use. While precise figures are not available for the average arrearage, the Real Estate Board has stated that in fiscal year 1975, 7.5 percent of all loft buildings were delinquent.[17] The Department of City Planning found that for loft buildings with legal or illegal use, the rate was 5 percent.[18] Using the 7.5 percent rate because it can take into account buildings that are more than one year overdue,[19] and the preconversion assessment used in earlier calculations, it is computed that

EXHIBIT V-13

TRANSFER PAYMENTS APPLICABLE TO COMMON MUNICIPAL SERVICES FISCAL YEAR 1977

	State Aid (millions)	*Federal Aid (millions)*	*Expenditure*	*Actual City Cost*
Municipal Parks	-	15	$ 88,914,000	$ 73,914,000
Public Safety	1	24	1,278,318,000	1,253,318,000
Sanitation	8	6	375,750,000	361,750,000
Health Services	69	15	238,298,000	154,298,000
Correction	1	4	101,143,000	96,143,000
Non-specified aid; all Other Common Municipal Services	134	159	1,597,719,000	1,304,719,000
TOTAL			$3,680,142,000	$ 3,244,142,000

1977 Per Capita Cost = $433 ($3,244,142,000 ÷ 7,490,690)

Source: The data on transfer payments for Fiscal Year 1977 came from "The Fiscal Observer," Volume II, Number 1 (January 19, 1978), p. 5.

Population estimate comes from Exhibit 24 in the population projection section of this study. (Attached as Exhibit V-13a for convenience.)

EXHIBIT V-13a

New York City Population by Age: 1970 to 1985

AGE CATEGORY	*1970*	*1975*	*1980*	*1985*
TOTAL	7,893,551	7,490,690	7,391,510	7,231,198
<5 years	613,738	496,813	519,854	527,984
5-14	1,257,374	1,041,381	832,302	742,535
15-24	1,258,373	1,296,348	1,273,863	1,084,822
25-34	1,075,505	1,347,501	1,568,478	1,620,530
35-44	911,264	771,696	875,558	1,163,284
45-54	937,952	839,820	701,291	585,808
55-64	888,614	771,803	698,555	619,076
65+	950,731	925,328	921,609	889,159

EXHIBIT V-14

DETERMINATION OF PRESENT VALUE OF COMMON MUNICIPAL SERVICE COSTS FOR AN INDUCED RESIDENT

$$\text{Present Value} = \sum_{t=o}^{24} \left(\frac{1.06}{1.08}\right)^t$$

t	*Per Capita Municipal Service Cost*	$(\frac{1.06}{1.08})^t$	*Present Value*
0	$433	1.0000	$433
1	433	.9815	425
2	433	.9633	417
3	433	.9455	409
4	433	.9280	402
5	433	.9109	394
6	433	.8940	387
7	433	.8775	380
8	433	.8612	373
9	433	.8453	366
10	433	.8297	359
11	433	.8143	353
12	433	.7993	346
13	433	.7845	340
14	433	.7699	333
15	433	.7557	327
16	433	.7417	321
17	433	.7280	315
18	433	.7145	309
19	433	.7013	304
20	433	.6883	298
21	433	.6756	293
22	433	.6631	287
23	433	.6508	282
24	433	.6388	277
TOTAL PRESENT VALUE (per capita):			$8,730

the city will collect $43 per unit in delinquent real estate taxes. Using the same delinquency rate and the average annual water charges for non-residential use, it is calculated that the city would collect $41 per unit in unpaid water charges. *The total from all these other sources of revenue is $343 per unit for all units converted (see Exhibit V-15).*

THE TOTAL COST OF THE J-51 PROGRAM

The preceding eight sections have detailed the calculations for revenues and costs that can be associated with the J-51 program. This section will total these revenues and costs, thereby determining the total fiscal impact of a unit converted under the provisions of the J-51 program.

Taxes are foregone, construction benefits are received, and other revenues are collected for every unit converted under the J-51 program. Several other costs and revenues are incurred or received only if a resident was induced to remain in the city by the converted unit. If the resident would have stayed in New York irrespective of the type of unit he could live in, the city has not realized any of the offsetting revenues, nor has it paid additionally for municipal services. Put more simply, the only additional revenues and costs that the city will realize from the conversion of a building are those that result from a resident's deciding to stay in the city, and from a small group of newcomers to the city who were lured there specifically by the availability of the new units and/or their attendant life style. While our survey quantified the latter number, it is relatively "soft" because the areas of uncertainty are substantial. In the interest of conservatism, therefore, the newcomers who claim to have come to New York City specifically because of converted apartments are excluded.

The quantification of the fiscal impact of the J-51 program as presented here turns on how many people are induced to stay in New York City. If nobody has been induced, the city will pay $6610 per unit that is converted.[20] In fact, this is a low expenditure for an increase in the city's housing stock when it is compared to the cost of constructing a new unit. But if it can be shown that some percentage of the residents were induced to stay because of the new type of unit available in a converted building, the city's expenditure

EXHIBIT V-15

OTHER REVENUES AND FEES PER CONVERTED UNIT

New York City Real Property Transfer Tax[1]	$ 75
New York City Mortgage Recording Tax[1]	116
J-51 Application and Filing Fees[1]	20
Building Department Fees[1]	48
Collection of Delinquent Real Estate Taxes[2] $6321 x 0.09 x 0.075 =	43
Collection of Delinquent Water Charges[3]	41
TOTAL OTHER REVENUES:	$343

[1]Real Estate Board, "Review of First Year's Experience Under the New J-51 Program," p. iv.

[2]Assessment rate of units before conversion, times tax rate, times 7.5 delinquency rate.

[3]Average annual water usage times 7.5 delinquency rate. The annual usage figure is an approximation based on the total number of establishments in New York City with a payroll (for services, wholesalers, and retail), and with at least twenty employees (for manufacturing) divided into the total nonresidential and nongovernmental water billing for the City of New York. The count of establishments is from County and City Data Book, 1972, a publication of the U.S. Department of Commerce; the yearly billing of non-residential, non-government accounts is from a telephone conversation with an officer of the Department of Water and Sewers, New York City.

is much lower.

Evidence from the interviews with residents living in over 500 converted units allows a measure of inducement. In response to the question:

> If an apartment similar to the one you live in now had not been available when you moved, would you have left the City?

7.7 percent of the residents said yes. This figure will be assumed to represent the percentage of residents of converted units that have been induced to stay in New York City. Using this assumption, all revenues and costs resulting from an induced resident will be multiplied by 7.7 percent, and the product will offset (or add to) the taxes foregone by the J-51 program. Conceptually, this is equivalent to saying that over the long run, 7.7 percent of the units converted will induce residents to stay in New York City, and the revenues from these residents will accrue to the city.

If 7.7 percent of the residents of converted units were induced to stay in New York City, the total impact of the J-51 program is to cost the city $5,971 (see Exhibit V-16).

SENSITIVITY ANALYSIS

All the calculations presented up to this point are based on explicit assumptions. Using these assumptions it can be shown that the J-51 program costs the city $5,971 per unit when the benefits and costs of induced residents are added to taxes foregone. It is very useful to consider how sensitive this figure is to changes in underlying assumptions. The important fact to keep in mind is that even without the offsetting benefits derived from the induced residents, the J-51 encouragement of conversion will cost the city $6,610 per unit.[21] This figure is so low compared to the cost of constructing a new unit that the J-51 program of tax abatements and exemptions could be supported without further calculation. However, the real cost to the city is substantially lower when the inducement effects are considered.

EXHIBIT V-16

Total Impact of the J-51 Program Per Unit

Item	*(Cost)/Revenue*
I. Taxes Foregone[1]	($7947)
II. Taxes Produced by Construction Spending[2]	237
III. Taxes Created through Multiplier Effects of Spending[3]	757
IV. Sales and Income Taxes Created by Induced Residents[4] ($10,243 x .077)	789
V. Tax Revenues Created by Multiplier Effects of Net Spending by Induced Residents[5] ($13,610 x .077)	1048
VI. Real Property Taxes Created by Expansion of Commercial Space Due to Spending by induced Residents[6] ($1901 x .077)	146
VII. Per Household Cost of Common Municipal Services for Induced Residents[7] ($17,460 x .077)	(1344)
VIII. Other Revenues and Fees[8]	343
TOTAL FISCAL IMPACT OF THE J-51 CONVERSION PROVISIONS:	($5971)

Notes: [1]From Exhibit V-1.
[2]From Exhibit V-2.
[3]From Exhibit V-3.
[4]From Exhibit V-8.
[5]From Exhibit V-9.
[6]From Exhibit V-11.
[7]From Exhibit V-14.
[8]From Exhibit V-15.

Change in Assumption: Qualifying Units

The preceding analysis assumed that all buildings with converted units qualified for the provisions of the J-51 program. The Department of City Planning has reported that only two-thirds of the projects eligible in the past have applied for benefits, and of these 90.9 percent were granted the tax benefits. If it were assumed that these same proportions were to apply in the future, it would mean that 60.1 percent of all units would be allowed tax abatements and exemptions. If a unit is converted and does not receive any J-51 tax savings, the city earns $13,594, discounted present value, over the 25 year economic life of the project (see Exhibit V-17). Assuming that induced residents will be apportioned no differently between qualifying and non-qualifying units, the per unit impact of the J-51 program is a gain to New York City of $1835 (see Exhibit V-18). It is interesting to consider what proportion of J-51 applicants could be accepted and have the net impact to the city be $0. Using reasoning similar to what is shown in Exhibit V-18, it can be shown that if the city grants 69.5 percent of the applications, it will neither gain nor lose money.

A parallel to this multiplier effect, i.e., non-J-51 construction or conversion stimulated by the abatement and exemption process, has not been appraised here. Its results, however, may be as significant as the new conventional development engendered in Greenwich Village because of the ambience of the older buildings which were revitalized within the area. The pump priming effect of the J-51 program in starting new construction and rehabilitation projects flowing in selected neighborhoods, projects that do not apply for J-51 benefits, may well be considerable, and means that the costs detailed here are the result of conservative estimates.

Change in Assumption: Induced Residents

The analysis which showed the total impact of the J-51 program to be $5,971 relied on the 7.7 percent response rate of conversion tenants who maintained their New York City residence because of the converted unit. What is the effect of this being overstated or understated? How many people would have to be induced for the J-51 program to pay for itself? As can be seen in Exhibit V-19, if the number of induced residents is

EXHIBIT V-17

Legal Conversions Without J-51 Benefits
(Constant Tax Rate)

t	*Assessment*	*Tax Rate*	*Tax*	$\frac{1}{1.08}^t$	*Discounted Present Value of Taxes Earned*
0	13096	.0900	1179	1.000	$1179
1	13096	.0900	1179	.9259	1092
2	13096	.0900	1179	.8573	1011
3	13096	.0900	1179	.7938	936
4	13096	.0900	1179	.7350	867
5	13096	.0900	1179	.6806	802
6	13096	.0900	1179	.6302	743
7	13096	.0900	1179	.5835	688
8	13096	.0900	1179	.5403	637
9	13096	.0900	1179	.5002	590
10	13096	.0900	1179	.4632	546
11	13096	.0900	1179	.4289	506
12	13096	.0900	1179	.3971	468
13	13096	.0900	1179	.3677	434
14	13096	.0900	1179	.3405	401
15	13096	.0900	1179	.3152	372
16	13096	.0900	1179	.2919	344
17	13096	.0900	1179	.2703	319
18	13096	.0900	1179	.2502	295
19	13096	.0900	1179	.2317	273
20	13096	.0900	1179	.2156	253
21	13096	.0900	1179	.1986	234
22	13096	.0900	1179	.1839	217
23	13096	.0900	1179	.1702	201
24	13096	.0900	1179	.1577	186
	TOTAL PRESENT VALUE:				$13,594

EXHIBIT V-18

J-51 PROGRAM FISCAL IMPACT WHEN 60.1 PERCENT OF CONVERTED UNITS QUALIFY FOR BENEFITS

FISCAL IMPACT OF CONVERTED UNIT UNDER J-51[1] = $5,971

FISCAL IMPACT OF CONVERTED UNIT, NO J-51 BENEFITS[2] = - $13,594

FISCAL IMPACT = 60.1% x (-$5,971) + 39.9% x ($13,594)
= (-$3,589) + ($5,424)

FISCAL IMPACT = $1835

Notes: [1]From Exhibit V-16.
[2]From Exhibit V-17.

EXHIBIT V-19

J-51 PROGRAM FISCAL IMPACT ASSUMING DIFFERENT PROPORTIONS OF INDUCED RESIDENTS

Item[1]	*(Cost)/Revenue*	*PERCENTAGE OF RESIDENTS INDUCED* 7.7%	3.9%	15.4%	79.7%
I. Taxes Foregone	($7947)	($7947)	($7947)	($7947)	($7947)
II. Taxes Produced by Construction Spending	237	237	237	237	237
III. Taxes Created through Multiplier Effects of Construction Spending	757	757	757	757	757
IV. Sales and Income Taxes Created by Induced Residents ($10,243 x) [1]	10,243	789	399	1577	8164
V. Tax Revenues Created by Multiplier Effects of Net Spending by Induced Residents ($13,609x) [1]	13,609	1048	531	2096	10,847
VI. Real Property Taxes Created by Expansion of Commercial Space Due to Spending by Induced Residents ($1901x) [1]	1901	146	74	293	1516
VII. Per Household Cost of Common Municipal Services for Induced Residents ($17,460x) [1]	(17,460)	(1344)	(681)	(2689)	(13,916)
VIII. Other Revenues and Charges	343	343	343	343	343
COST TO CITY		($5971)	($6287)	($5333)	$0
Percentage Difference in Number of Induced Residents		-	-50%	+100%	+935%
Percentage Difference in Costs from Survey Results of Induced Residents (which showed 7.7% were induced.)		-	+5.3%	-10.7%	-100%

Note: [1]The "x" shown in items IV, V, VI, and VII is the percentage of residents induced to stay in New York City.

half what the survey found, the net fiscal impact of the tax inducements is a $6287 total cost; if the number of induced residents is double what the survey found, the fiscal impact is a $5333 loss; and finally, the city would have to have induced 79.7 percent of the conversion residents to stay in New York City in order for the program to pay for itself.

SUMMARY

Several rationales for continuing the J-51 program were offered at the begining of this section. Briefly, these were improved neighborhoods, decreased vacancies in existing structures, better maintained buildings, and an increased housing supply.

Even with these important reasons for continuing the tax inducements for conversions, it is still important to the city to know how much the tax inducements will cost. The discussion included in this chapter shows that the greatest possible cost to New York City is $7947 per unit, the present discounted value of property tax revenues over the economic life of the conversion (25 years). This highest cost occurs if a conversion was granted J-51 benefits, but would have occurred without the tax inducements.

A slightly lower cost of $6610 per unit is the price the city will pay if a converted unit houses a citizen who would have remained in New York City regardless of the type of unit available, but if the conversion would not have occurred without J-51 benefits.

The lowest cost possible to the city is $5971 per unit when the converted units induce 7.7 percent of the residents to stay in the city, and when the conversion would not have occurred without the J-51 program.

Given these figures, and given the reasons cited above for supporting the conversion activity, it seems that the investment made by the city in J-51 bax benefits will be well spent. Neighborhoods will be revived, buildings will be maintained, and commercial activities will increase -- and all for a price that at the highest is $7947 per unit.

FOOTNOTES

1. Construction spending is created when a commercial building is converted to residential use.

2. Multiplier effects result from the fact that an initial injection of spending goes into the pockets of households and firms, and that some portion is re-spent. The cycle repeats itself, although each round is smaller and smaller because of leakages into savings, taxes, or spending outside the local economy.

3. The proportions spent for materials and labor for a conversion are based on a report by the Real Estate Board of New York, Inc., entitled "Review of the First Year's Experience Under the New J-51 Program."

4. Construction spending is created when a commercial building is converted to residential use.

5. The 0.4 marginal propensity to consume locally is an estimate which takes into account the leakages from the spending stream through savings of households and firms, through various tax payments, and through spending outside the local economy. The estimate is very conservative.

6. This 8 percent figure is based on analysis of the household budget presented in Exhibit V-4. Sales and income taxes amount to something less than 2 percent of the household income. If property taxes equalling approximately 25 percent of rent were paid, then the tax contribution would be about 8 percent of income.

7. This is a conservative statement of the effect of inducing a resident to remain in New York City because so many (35 percent) of the respondents are self-employed. This means that if the city had not induced the resident to stay, it would not only have lost most of the family spending shown in Exhibit V-4, but would as well have lost business spending associated with the resident. In the interest of simplicity and conservatism, the business spending is not quantified.

8. Vacation transportation is included in the miscellaneous taxable item. If a ticket is purchased within the city for a vacation elsewhere, then the city sales tax is paid.

9. While this same family is not likely to remain in the unit or have similar expenditure patterns over twenty-five years, it is assumed that a similar family will take occupancy and be in the same life cycle stage that the original family was in when it took occupancy. This change in tenantry should repeat itself over the economic life of the dwelling unit.

10. This is equal to income ($21,783) less sales taxes to the city and state for expenditures in the city ($400), less expenditures outside the city ($504 for food and miscellaneous taxable items, $53 for gasoline), less spending which would have taken place even if the household did not live in the city ($5401 x .15 = $810), less other gasoline taxes (500 gallons x $.12 = $60), less savings ($1,223), less federal, state, and city income taxes ($5,036). This leaves a net injection of local spending, exclusive of all taxes of $13,697.

11. This assumes that eight cents on the dollar ends up in sales, income, or property taxes. This is based on an analysis of the estimated household budget in Exhibit V-4. Sales and income taxes amount to somewhat less than 2 percent of income. If property taxes were fully paid, the figures would rise to 8 percent.

12. Changes in sales, income, and property tax rates are ignored over the period so that multiplier effects on taxes will be understated.

13. "Long-run" refers to a time at which the firm will be able to expand capacity. It is not so much a time dimension as a measure of the firm's flexibility to vary production. If expansion of space coincides with expansion of residential space, then the long run begins when the program begins.

14. Transportation expenditures are excluded from the analysis.

15. Even if this additional retail volume does not generate additional space to be taxed, its results would

in the long run, be equivalent in reinforcing the economic viability and value of existing facilities. Although spending by the household is expected to increase 6 percent per year, it is not assumed that this will result in an expansion of commercial space beyond the initial adjustment.

16. Real Estate Board of New York City, Inc., "Review of the First Year's Experience Under the New J-51 Program," p. iv.

17. Statement of Edward R. Potter of the Real Estate Board before the City Planning Commission, February 25, 1976.

18. Telephone conversation with Mike Levine, Department of City Planning, December 21, 1977.

19. It can be assumed that if the delinquent bills are extreme (to have accumulated over several years), a developer would choose another building.

20. This figure is the sum of the tax revenues foregone ($7947) less the taxes produced by construction spending ($237), less the taxes created through multiplier effects of construction spending ($757), less other revenues collected ($343).

21. This figure is computed as described in footnote 20.

Chapter 6

CONCLUSIONS

While housing by itself cannot revive New York City's economy, it can be argued that much of the city's appeal as a business location has been lost by its failure to offer reasonably priced housing appropriate for prospective businessmen and their employees. The loss of appeal has several effects. More and more middle income residents leave, although they continue to work in the city. In turn, the departure of these residents means the loss of customers for the city's retailing and service industries.

New York City has long recognized these equations for middle class departure, and has tried many subsidies to foster housing alternatives within its boundaries. These subsidies are an attempt to induce middle-income residents to come to or to stay in the city, and thereby to allow the city to salvage some part of its eroding tax base. Section 421 of the Real Property Law is such a subsidy.

There is now a new approach to housing subsidy which marries the aforementioned salvaging operation to a new salvaging, the conversion of idle commercial and industrial space to residential use. By capitalizing on the healthy market for converted buildings, the city hopes not only to increase the housing supply attractive to middle class tenants, it hopes as well to recycle the old buildings, thereby improving neighborhoods and decreasing vacancies and tax delinquencies among existing structures. Section J-51 of the Administrative Code provides this subsidy for conversions.

The research described in this volume intended to clarify several aspects of the city's attempts to maintain its middle class population and to revitalize neighborhoods. Specifically, the residents of converted buildings were surveyed to find out what kind of housing is available in these recycled structures, and also to find out if this housing is appealing to middle class New Yorkers. A similar survey was conducted of the residents of new apartment buildings which receive Section 421 tax benefits. Here the intention was to discern differences between people who live in converted buildings and people who have chosen more traditional apartment buildings. In both these surveys the residents were asked questions about how much inducement they feel to stay in the city, and how satisfied they are with their current living situation. A final survey, intended to measure the likelihood of suburban workers' moving to the city, asked railroad commuters about their uses of and attitudes toward New York City.

The results of all three surveys provide a detailed accounting of who the city is providing tax subsidies for, how strong an attachment to New York City there is among these residents, and how many suburban commuters are likely to move to the city. A final part of the research described here analyzed the costs the city will bear by using the J-51 tax benefits schedule to encourage conversions.

The most important findings from these several research activities, described in detail in the preceding five chapters, are as follows:

CONVERTED BUILDINGS

The Recycled Buildings and Dwellings

1. The conversion of buildings from a commercial or industrial use to residential occupancy has been predominantly illegal. The recycled buildings were designed to house non-residential endeavors, and their conversion is illegal either because they are in districts where residential use is prohibited or because they do not meet city standards for inhabitation. Only 10 percent of the conversions are legal, and it has been estimated that there are about 10,000 converted units in New York City.

2. Coversions are of two types. First is conventionally converted space, in which the owner has made a considerable investment in improving space. Once inside the dwelling unit, a tenant would find the small size and appurtenances very similar to an ordinary apartment building. All conventional conversions are legal, and the units created are called converted apartments.

   Second is unconventionally converted space, in which the owner offers a tenant open, undifferentiated space and typically does not provide necessities such as kitchens and bathrooms. In general, the owner has made no investment in the conversion and the tenants make all improvements. This type of recycled unit is popularly known as a residential loft, and the lofts are predominantly illegal.

3. The average converted apartment offers 600 square feet of space, and rents for $393 per month, or $.64 per square foot per month.

4. The average residential loft offers nearly 2100 square feet of space, and rents for $392 per month, or $.19 per square foot per month. The tenants of these large, unimproved spaces spend an average of $7108 on the units for necessary facilities. These figures are for legal and illegal residents.

5. The illegal residents of lofts typically spend about $390 per month for units that are 2343 square feet in area, and invest $6248 on improvements. The attractions of the large and flexible spaces are sufficient that residents are willing to risk living in and improving places to which they have no claim at law.

The Neighborhoods that Contain Recycled Buildings

1. Converted buildings can be found in two types of neighborhoods. First are conventional neighborhoods, areas that have long been residential, and that offer the typical appurtenant facilities such as schools, parks, and trees. Second are unconventional neighborhoods, areas that have traditionally been commercial, and that offer facilities accessory to trade such as loading docks, but that offer few conveniences for residents.

2. When conversion residents of each type of neighborhood were asked to comment on the area, their responses were remarkably similar. High percentages of residents of both types of areas regarded their neighborhoods positively.

3. Although residents of unconventional neighborhoods receive fewer city services and endure greater inconvenience in obtaining personal goods and services such as groceries, their sense of the importance of city and personal services is no different from what is reported by residents of conventional areas. But the converted units available in the unconventional neighborhoods offer amenities that seem to outweigh the scarcity of city and personal conveniences.

The Residents of Converted Units

1. Converted space is a major attraction to newcomers to New York. More than 30 percent of the occupants moved to their apartments from addresses outside New York City. At

the same time, the availability of this housing does not seem to play a critical role in keeping people as city residents. Ninety-two percent of the respondents indicated they would have stayed in New York regardless of whether this special kind of housing had been available.

2. People attracted to converted units are young, well paid, and extremely well educated. The median age of conversion residents is 31.8 years (the city-wide median is 44.4 years); the median household income is $21,783 per year (the city-wide median is $9,255); and 74.2 percent of the residents have at least a college degree (10.6 percent of the residents of New York City have an equal achievement).

3. The high educational attainments and the high salaries imply the highly specialized occupations of the conversion residents. Indeed, 56 percent of the converted unit occupants are employed in managerial, professional, and technical positions (for the whole city, 21 percent have these occupations). The conversions house an extremely high proportion of artists, 24 percent. Forty-five percent of the illegal residents say they are artists.

4. Large size and attractive, flexible space seem to be the major inducements and satisfaction for people living in converted dwellings. Convenience (proximity to work and shopping) and price are significantly less important as reasons for living in this new kind of housing.

5. Residents of lofts plan to stay in them an average of eight years, while people living in the more ordinary conversions foresee staying there only three years.

6. Few converted apartments are owned by the residents. People who own the lofts intend to stay there 12 years.

7. The residents as a group are well satisfied with their housing, and would like to stay in New York City. Using a scale from 1 to 5, on which 5 is very satisfied, the residents reported their satisfaction as 4; the large majority would choose to live in the converted unit again. While more than half the residents said they considered living in an apartment building at the time they found the converted space, less than 14 percent reported considering a move to the suburbs. Only 28 percent of the residents of illegally converted lofts considered any other kind of housing. This is probably due in some part to the high proportion of artists who live in the illegal space because they need the sizable floor area for their artistic pursuits.

NEW APARTMENT BUILDINGS

The Section 421 Buildings and Apartments

1. From the inception of the Section 421 Program in 1971 until July, 1977, 18,280 units were completed. An additional 11,267 units have received preliminary certification to be constructed.

2. The type of building receiving Section 421 benefits varies greatly by borough. In Manhattan, 55 percent of all units are in buildings that contain at least 250 apartments; in all the other boroughs there is a substantial number of six-family structures and only 21 percent of the units are in large buildings.

3. The median monthly rent for a Section 421 apartment in Manhattan is $506; in the other boroughs it is $321. These medians and the distribution of rents charged indicate that the cost of Section 421 apartments is in the highest ranges of rents found in New York City.

4. The tenants of Section 421 units choose to live in them chiefly because of their amenities, their size, their convenience, or their price. Apartments which have a view and buildings with security systems are nearly three times as important to Manhattan residents as to residents of the other four boroughs.

5. Nearly three quarters of the respondents living in Section 421 apartments think that their neighborhoods are pleasant. Although four-tenths of the residents do not think any additional city services are necessary to improve their neighborhood, approximately 30 percent think that street cleaning and repair, and garbage collection should be improved.

The Residents of Section 421 Buildings

1. These newly-constructed buildings attract about 45 percent of their residents from places other than New York City. However, the units do not seem to provide the most important inducement to stay in the city, since 86 percent of the residents would have stayed in New York City if a similar unit had not been available.

2. People attracted to Section 421 units are young, well-paid, and highly educated. While in the city as a whole 21 percent of the workers are employed in professional, technical, managerial, administrative, or proprietary jobs, 72 percent of the Section 421 residents pursue these occupations. The median age is 33.6 years, much lower than the citywide median of 44.4 years. Finally, the median household income is $24,268, about two and a half times the city-wide median of $9,255.

3. There are usually two adults in the household and only 17 percent of the households have children. In 41 percent of the units, the household is headed by a woman.

4. The typical residents of Section 421 buildings in Manhattan are somewhat younger, are better educated, are more often employed in highly-skilled jobs, and earn more money than residents of these buildings sited in the other boroughs.

5. As a group, the residents are fairly well satisfied. Using a scale from one to five, on which five is very satisfied, the mean level of satisfaction is 3.8. Residents in Manhattan are somewhat more satisfied (3.9) than outer borough tenants (3.6). An additional indication of satisfaction is that nearly three-quarters of the tenants would choose again to live in their unit.

6. The respondents living in Section 421 apartments intend to stay in them an average of 2.4 years. Eighty-one percent plan to stay less than 3 years; and of these, a little more than half anticipate moving to another location in New York City, while 20 percent intend to move away from the New York City Metropolitan Region entirely.

7. When confronted with the possibility of greatly escalated housing costs, the largest portion of residents said they would remain in the city and look for cheaper housing. From this and other measures of satisfaction and inducement, it could be inferred that Section 421 buildings provide an attractive housing option, but that their location is their most important attribute, particularly in Manhattan.

COMPARISON OF CONVERTED AND NEW BUILDINGS

1. There are significant differences between Section 421 buildings in Manhattan and in the other four boroughs, and all the converted buildings under study are in Manhattan. For the sake of comparability, the discussion will be limited to buildings located in Manhattan.

2, All Section 421 Buildings (in Manhattan) are new, and most of them contain more than 250 apartments. The converted buildings are older; their architecture represents the fashion of their day and heralds their former commercial or industrial use. Converted apartments (conventionally converted spaces) typically are in buildings with 100-150 units; lofts (unconventionally converted spaces) are typically in buildings with only 12 units.

3. Lofts offer floor space of 2100 square feet and have median monthly rents of $392; converted apartments have only 610 square feet and median rents of $393; and Section 421 units contain 875 square feet and the median monthly cost is $506. The monthly price per square foot is about the same for the latter two types of dwellings ($.58 for Section 421 units, $.64 for converted apartments), and nearly three times the price for lofts ($.19 per square foot per month). (See text for the sample limitations.) The citywide median rent was $171 in 1975.

4. The largest proportion of residents of all three types of units appears to be able to choose a place to live in New York City based on some physical quality of a particular unit. Except for artists' requiring large spaces at low per square foot prices, most of the residents appear to be able to afford to live wherever the amenities and the location suit them.

5. Although the residents of all three types of units are considerably younger than typical New York City renters, the people living in converted apartments are the youngest (median ages are: Section 421 units, 33.6 years; lofts, 34.0 years; converted apartments, 29.6 years; for New York City, median age for renters was 44.4 years in 1975).

6. The residents of lofts, converted apartments, and Section 421 units are typically much better educated than average New York City residents, so that the differences among the residents of new types of units are of little importance. In New York City, only 10.6 percent of the population has completed college; however, 80.5 percent of loft residents, 69.2 percent of converted apartment residents, and 77.7 percent of Section 421 residents have equivalent attainments.

7. Aside from the high percentage of artists residing in lofts, the occupations pursued by residents in all three types of units are quite similar, and markedly different from those pursued by typical New York City residents. For example, the highly-skilled jobs (professional/technical, artist, manager, administrator, proprietor) are held by 23.5 percent of all New Yorkers; however, they are held by 76.5 percent of Section 421 residents, 75.2 percent of converted apartment residents, and 86.9 percent of loft residents.

8. Median annual household incomes similarly are much higher than for typical New York City households ($9,255). The two surveys found that loft households earn $22,253, converted apartment households earn $21,479, and Section 421 households earn $24,268 per year.

9. The most noteworthy point to be made about these comparisons of residents of Section 421 units, converted apartments, and lofts, is that the ways in which they differ from one another are small compared to how they all differ from residents of New York City in general.

10. The levels of satisfaction do not vary noticeably among the residents of the three new types of housing. However, the residents of lofts intend to stay in their units much longer than the other residents, and nearly all of the loft residents would choose to live there again.

11. Nearly a third of the dissatisfied residents of Section 421 housing intend to look for suburban housing next, perhaps an implication that they consider their unit the ultimate alternative in New York City, and that dissatisfaction forces them to look outside the city. For the most part, dissatisfied residents of both types of units in converted buildings intend to look elsewhere in the city for a new units.

12. Despite the dissatisfaction evident in point 12 above, the large majority of respondents living in all three types of units have neither considered moving to the suburbs nor would have left the city had a similar unit not been available.

13. Residents of lofts feel the greatest attachment to New York City. Few of these residents either considered moving to the suburbs or would have left the city if a similar unit had not been available.

14. By encouraging conversion and new construction, New York City is adding attractive housing options to its stock of dwelling units. These are providing homes for young, well-educated, highly paid tenants, the residents who make important contributions of their skills and their spending to the city's economy.

COMMUTERS TO NEW YORK CITY: POTENTIAL CITY RESIDENTS?

1. The median age of the commuters is 43.8 years. Typically, the commuter is very well educated (75 percent have at least finished college), works in a highly-skilled occupation (72 percent have white collar jobs), and is very well paid (median annual household income is $36,046).

2. Over half the commuters have lived in New York City. Their reasons for having moved out of the city are that they wanted to own a house (27 percent), wanted to enjoy suburban amenities (27 percent), or wanted to live in an environment more suitable for children than the city (19 percent).

3. Although the average commuting time is two and a half hours each day, the respondents are very well contented. When asked to rate satisfaction, using a scale from 1 to 5 on which 5 is very satisfied, the average rating was 4.2. The satisfaction is also apparent in the commuters' intentions to remain in their residence an average of 12 years.

4. Outdoor recreation and relaxing at home are the most favored leisure time activities of these suburbanites. Dining out and going to movies or plays follow, and least important is going to museums.

5. On the average, the commuters go to New York City once a month for some kind of entertainment.

6. Eleven percent of the commuters intend to move to New York City, but their plans are focused about eight years in the future. Only 13 percent of them know of and would like to live in a converted building.

7. Asked to consider the hypothetical situation that they would have to move to New York City in the next year, the commuters were queried about which borough they would prefer, the kind of housing they would seek, and how much they would expect to have to pay for it.

The overwhelming choice was an apartment or brownstone in Manhattan, and on the average the respondents expected to pay approximately 12 percent more for a place in the city than for their current residence.

8. Commuters find New York City most enjoyable for the cultural activities there, for the excitement or ambience of the city, and for the entertainment to be found. Interestingly, the pattern of responses does not vary according to how the commuters have ranked the importance of leisure time activities. For example, people for whom going to museums is not very important do not mention the enjoyment of these cultural activities any less often than people who rate going to museums as most important. A possible explanation is that for many commuters it is important that in the city there be cultural activities, regardless of the commuter's use of these activities.

9. The most disliked aspects of New York City are filth and pollution (27 percent), crime (25 percent), and crowding or congestion (22 percent).

10. When asked what they would do if their monthly housing costs were to double, 57 percent said they would pay the increase. Only 3 percent would move to New York City.

11. The intention to move to the city that 11 percent of the commuters report does not seem to be predicated on an intense desire to be there, a desire born from a mass of dissatisfactions with the suburbs. It is a calmer desire, one not very apt to be inflamed even by the instance of greatly increased suburban costs of housing.

12. The most important distinguishing characteristics between commuters who do and do not plan to move to New York City are their incomes and the frequency with which they come to the city for entertainment. Suburbanites who intend to move to the city have median household incomes of $48,013, nearly 40 percent higher

than the median reported by those with no such intentions ($34,841 per year). And the commuters who plan a move to the city come there twice as often for entertainment than do the suburbanites without plans to move.

13. The personal characteristics and the attitudes toward New York, summarized above for all the railroad commuters, are virtually invariant when all these respondents are partitioned according to their age, to their having or not having children, to the state in which they live, and even according to whether or not they plan to move to the city. They are, in short, a very homogeneous group with respect to the questions that this study asked.

14. There is little evidence among the railroad commuters of a strong desire to move to New York City.

THE COST OF ENCOURAGING NEW AND SALVAGED HOUSING

1. Other studies have shown that the costs of the Section 421 tax benefits are exceeded by the benefits derived by the city from the residents of the new apartment buildings.

2. Briefly, the benefits of encouraging the conversion of idle commercial buildings are improved neighborhoods, decreased vacancies and tax delinquencies among existing structures better maintained buildings, and an increased housing supply.

3. Interviews conducted with conversion residents showed that the median rent paid was $375 per month in buildings that had J-51 tax benefits, and were 8 percent higher, or $405, in the buildings that had no tax advantages.

4. Assuming that the economic life of a converted unit is 25 years, that the property tax rate will remain at 9 percent of assessed value, and that an 8 percent discount rate is proper, it will cost the city an average of $6,610, present discounted value, per unit, to encourage conversions with the J-51 tax benefits.

5 Among the residents of converted units, 7.7 percent said that they would have left the city if there had not been available a recycled unit. If conversions continue to induce residents to stay in the city in the same proportions that have been induced thus far, the $6,610 per unit cost quoted above can be reduced to $5,971 per unit because of induced resident spending.

The fact that people who plan to move to New York City are so very affluent could be interpreted to mean that those less affluent think the cost of living in the city is prohibitive. Along this line of reasoning it is important to recall that the commuters participating in the survey predicted having to pay more for accommodations in the city than they pay in the suburbs. It could be argued that for the move to the city to be a strong competitor with remaining in the suburbs, the price of housing in the two places cannot overwhelmingly favor remaining outside the city. The implication of this argument is that since the commuters appear to favor high-rise apartments, the Section 421 benefits should be extended since they provide rent reductions and thereby increase the attraction of New York City to its suburban workers.

However, the most likely future market for housing in New York City is not the suburban commuters. It is the young, highly-skilled and professional worker who wants to live in the city for the kind of sophisticated life to be found there. The most successful policy that the city can pursue is one that will keep these people within its jurisdiction. As detailed in Chapter 3, the housing portion of such a policy would attempt to provide a diversity of housing options in a variety of neighborhoods. Such a policy would mean that when a lease expires for one apartment, the tenant can find housing with similar amenities without having to move to the suburbs.

Volume II of this study projects the population of New York City for 1980 and 1985. According to these projections, the city can expect increasing numbers of households even as the population declines. These additional households will for the most part contain individuals who are between 25 and 44 years of age. The structure of the projected new households will be mostly primary individuals; there will be fewer husband-wife families. In short, the projected new households are quite similar to those that find converted buildings and Section 421 buildings attractive.

Some urban observers have found evidence that suburban dwellers may be attracted to moving to central cities because of four factors. First, increased fuel costs and the uncertain future quantities of fuel have improved the locational advantages of central-city areas. Second, environmental concerns have constrained suburban development by making it more difficult and costly than it has been before. Third, the cost of constructing and servicing new housing has increased extravagantly, making new suburban homes less attractive to homebuyers and taxpayers. And finally, the personal characteristics of metropolitan populations have changed; there are larger proportions of childless and single-person households than before, households for which better schools and improved play areas are irrelevant. Of more interest are jobs, entertainment, and other cultural divertissements.

The factors that seem to indicate increased central city attractiveness do not seem to have had much effect on suburban commuters. However, they may be important as inhibitors to city residents contemplating a move to the suburbs. New York City can provide an enhanced competitive position by providing an ample supply of housing that the potential suburbanites prefer.

Appendixes

APPENDIX A
REHABILITATION PROGRAMS SPONSORED BY NEW YORK CITY

J-51 Tax Abatement and Exemption

This program, defined in Section J-51 - 2.5 of the Administrative Code of New York City, was enacted in 1955 to encourage the conversion of rooming houses by the installation of private bathrooms and kitchens. It has been expanded into a program for the rehabilitation of old buildings. The most recent expansion of the program is to give benefits to owners who convert commercial space to residential use (see Chapters 1, 2, 3, and 5 of this study).

The benefits for rehabilitation are in two parts, exemption and abatement:

Exemption: When and if the assessed valuation is increased due to improvements, the property will be exempted from all taxes that result from the increased valuation for 12 years. (Taxes will be computed on the old assessment, but these will be abated by the second part of the program.)

Abatement: Abatements of yearly taxes for 9-20 years are allowed, accumulating until taxes equalling 90 percent of the reasonable cost of rehabilitation (certified by the Housing and Development Administration) have been abated. The maximum annual abatement that is allowed is 8.3 percent of the certified cost of rehabiliation.

Mini-Loan Program

The funds for this program come from the Community Development Block Grant. As of 1977, a total of $4,000,000 was slated for this program. Mini-loans are made when an owner cannot get private financing, and are to be used for major systems repair. The maximum loan is $3,000 per unit and $75,000 per building; the interest rate is 3 percent.

Office of Code Enforcement

This office (part of the Department of Development in the Housing and Development Administration) gets approximately $2,000,000 in Community Development Funds for its Emergency Repair Program.

The Emergency Repair Program involves a workshop in which city workers are trained to do repair work on buildings. Some of the "emergency repair" work is done by this city crew and the rest is contracted out. After the work is completed the city will either bill the landlord, file a lien against the property, or ask the tenants to pay for the work (and allow them to deduct the payment from the rent due the landlord).

The more routine operations of the Office of Code Enforcement are predicated on complaint. Following a complaint made by a tenant, an inspector will be sent to the building. He will be responsible for inspecting the conditions complained of and all violations which he may reasonably be expected to see in the course of his inspection of the complaint. He will not be responsible for inspecting any other violations in the building.

After the landlord is given a reasonable period of time to correct the violations, there is a routine re-inspection to ensure their correction. For this inspection, the inspector will have a list of all pending violations on a building, and must therefore check the entire building.

The cost of Code Enforcement is 50 percent reimbursable by the state. However, the reimbursements are based on a projected estimate of costs for the year rather than on actual costs. Therefore, the state reimbursement level usually is less than half the costs. The budget in 1977 was about $12 million.

Participation Loan Program for Rehabilitation

The money for this program comes from the Community Development grant, and then is combined with private funding. In 1977 the amount from the grant was $13 million. Under the program, the city provides 40 percent of a loan for rehabilitation at 1 percent interest, and savings associations participating in the program provide 60 percent of the loan at conventional interest rates. A commercial bank does the construction financing.

The program is constrained by where the banks will not participate. Therefore, it does not solve the problems of certain areas of New York City where banks refuse to participate unless they already hold the mortgage for another building in the area.

REMIC (Rehabilitation Mortgage Insurance Corporation)

REMIC insures conventional mortgages on residential properties in specific Neighborhood Preservation Areas such as Washington Heights in Manhattan. These areas are suitable for REMIC because the housing stock is essentially sound, although additional capital is needed. REMIC is a small insurance program of limited resources. As of 1977, it had reserves of $9,000,000.

Section 421 Partial Tax Exemption

Section 421 of the Real Property Tax Law offers a partial tax exemption for rehabilitation and for new construction. Its use for encouraging new construction is reported in Chapter 2 of the text.

Although Section 421 benefits can be used for rehabilitation, the J-51 program provides greater benefits. 421 does not provide for an abatement, and only allows a maximum exemption from the increased valuation of 50 percent over ten years. Therefore, few owners use this program for rehabilitation.

SHIP (Small Home Improvement Program)

This program uses Community Development funds to rehabilitate vacant homes in areas that have not completely deteriorated. The program is restricted to 1-4 family homes.

If the city agrees to rehabilitate an area, the federal government provides FHA 203 insurance and the city buys the properties from HUD (the price is generally the liens and taxes on the property + $500). *In rem* (city-owned) properties are also used. The owners of vacant buildings that have not been foreclosed are given 312 federal loans. The city then rehabilitates the houses and sells them.

In order to buy the homes, private homeowners must obtain permanent financing. The city will arrange such permanent financing with local institutions. SHIP is a revolving fund. As homeowners obtain permanent financing and buy the homes from the city, the money is then available for new rehabilitation projects.

APPENDIX B
METHODOLOGY

The material presented in Chapters 1, 2, 3, and 4 is based on the results of three surveys. The design of each of these surveys is described below:

SURVEY I: CONVERTED BUILDINGS

Careful consideration of the phenomenon of residential use of a building that had once had a commercial or industrial function yields two variables of importance. First is the way in which the building has been converted. The owner or developer of one of these buildings can either offer space that he has done little or nothing to - leaving many if not all necessary changes to the discretion of tenants, or he can actually convert the space into apartments before offering them to the market. In the first instance, the tenant finds a large amount of undifferentiated space and typically has to provide necessities such as a kitchen, bathroom, or dividing walls. In the second instance, the tenant finds an apartment developed much like any other apartment in New York City, although amenities such as high ceilings and large windows might be included because of the nature of the building before conversion. The important distinction between these two development options and other types of housing is that the units under study are in buildings converted from a nonresidential use.

The two options for offering units in converted buildings will be called "converted apartments" when the owner has created fairly standard units, and "residential lofts" when the owner has offered space with little or no improvements.*

---

*The reader is cautioned to remember that this distinction is being made between residents of converted buildings, and that in a sense all the respondents live in unconventional structures.

The second important variable in thinking about this new type of housing is the neighborhood in which the converted building is located. If it is sited in an area which has traditionally been residential, it can be said to be in a "conventional neighborhood." However, if it is in a location traditionally commercial or industrial, the building will be said to be in an "unconventional neighborhood."

Using these two descriptive variables, it is possible to divide the residents of converted buildings into four groups, as follows:

Group 1 Converted Apartments in a Conventional Neighborhood

Group 2: Converted Apartments in an Unconventional Neighborhood

Group 3: Residential Lofts in a Conventional Neighborhood

Group 4: Residential Lofts in an Unconventional Neighborhood

Dividing conversion residents in this way allows a responsible interpretation of the variation in satisfaction and desires that can be found among the respondents.

The method used to study the people living in converted buildings was a comprehensive survey in which residents were asked questions pertaining to seven categories of interest. These were personal characteristics; general residence data (current unit and previous location); dwelling unit characteristics; building characteristics; neighborhood characteristics; reasons for living in the particular unit and neighborhood; and satisfaction. The responses tell who the respondents are, why they live where they do, where they came from, what services their neighborhoods afford, what amenities are available in their unit and buildings, and how satisfied they are with their accommodations.

Buildings were chosen by the New York City Planning Department for inclusion in each of the four categories. During the eight week period from August 10 through September 29, 1977, interviews were conducted with occupants of 502 individual units in 52 buildings.

Approximately half of the interviews were in person, and the other half were conducted over the telephone. Interviews were conducted during weekdays, on week ends, and in the evening, so that there need be no concern about their reflecting only a small subset of people who happen to be at home during tightly circumscribed times of the day.

In any research, the question of the reliability of a sample is basic to an interpretation of results. At the time this study was designed, there were no figures on the extent of residential use, legal and illegal, of commercial space. This was not particularly troublesome, since a sample that numbers 500 units and that has been chosen in a deliberate manner is large enough to give reasonably reliable results. In the time since the interviews were conducted, the Department of City Planning of New York City has completed a study which quantifies the conversion activity, and shows that 90 percent of the conversions completed thus far have been illegal. This is much higher than the 20 percent shown in the sample. However, the underrepresentation of illegal tenants does not affect any discussion which specifically differentiates between legal and illegal buildings, units, and residents. Any caveats necessary for proper interpretation of results have been included throughout Chapters 1 and 3 in appropriate places.

SURVEY II: NEW APARTMENT BUILDINGS

The chief concern in designing the study of residents of Section 421 housing was that a complete picture of the tenancy be drawn. Because of the wide variety of locales (all five boroughs) and the variability in unit configurations (from small, six family structures to complexes with hundreds of units), a sampling frame that fairly represented the total universe was needed.

Working from data supplied by the Housing and Development Administration, Partial Tax Exemption Program office, the total universe of units was first narrowed to those which had been constructed prior to January 1, 1977, to insure that sample buildings were occupied. From the resulting list of 204 buildings with 17,837 units, a sample of 45 buildings was randomly chosen. The sample contains 22 percent of the total number of structures, 20 percent of the units completed prior to January 1, 1977, and is representative of every type of building in each borough that receives Section 421 benefits.

From the Cole Household Directories a list of residents for each of the sample buildings was obtained. Because of vacancies and unlisted numbers, 30 percent of all the units had numbers unavailable from the directories. Using the phone lists, interviewers contacted the residents of the Section 421 buildings during late September and early October, 1977. The interviews were administered between the hours of 6-10 p.m. Monday through Friday, from 2-10 p.m. on Saturday and 10 a.m. - 10 p.m. on Sunday. A total of 505 interviews were obtained.

The residents of the Section 421 buildings were asked many of the same questions posed to residents of converted buildings. Specifically, the new apartment building dwellers were asked about their personal characteristics; general residence data; dwelling unit, building, and neighborhood characteristics; reasons for living where they do; and their satisfaction. In addition, the Section 421 residents were asked about their interest in living in converted buildings.

SURVEY III: RAILROAD COMMUTERS

A random sample of railroad commuters was chosen for a telephone survey. During the week of March 5 through 11, 1974, one thousand commuters were contacted, and 678 interviews were completed. These interviews provide information which includes personal characteristics, reasons for living in the suburbs, and attitudes toward New York City in general and toward living there in particular.

The 678 interviews were made with residents of New York, New Jersey and Connecticut in approximately the same proportions that all rail commuters from the three states are distributed, as the following chart shows:

	All Rail Commuters	Sample
New York	70.9%	63.1%
New Jersey	22.0	24.8
Connecticut	8.0	12.1

APPENDIX C
NEIGHBORHOODS WHICH CONTAIN CONVERTED BUILDINGS

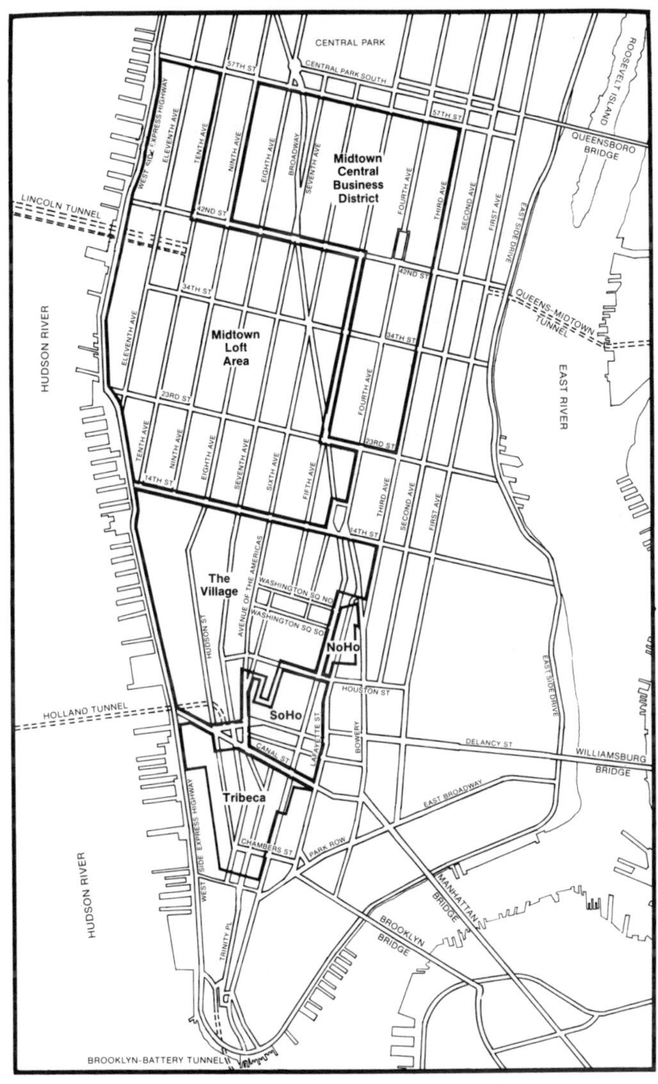

APPENDIX D
OCCUPATIONS

The following list summarizes the definitions used by the U.S. Bureau of the Census to classify occupations, the list used in this study to classify the responses of the respondents in the three surveys.

Professional or technical - accountants, architects, engineers, lawyers, librarians, physicians, teachers, social scientists, life and physical scientists, nurses.

manager, administrator, proprietor - bank officers, buyers (wholesale and retail trade), funeral directors, sales managers, school administrators.

sales worker - advertising agents, insurance agents, brokers, underwriters, stocks and bond salesmen, real estate agents and brokers.

clerical - bank tellers, cashiers, file clerks, office machine operators, secretaries, typists, receiptionists.

craftsmen, foremen - carpenters, heavy equipment operators, electricians, jewelers, machinists, mechanics, plumbers.

operatives - garage workers, textile operatives, welders and flame cutters, milliners, clothing ironers and pressers.

laborer - animal caretakers, garbage collectors, longshoremen, teamsters, warehousemen.

service worker - cleaning service workers, food service workers, waiters, health service workers, barber, airline stewardesses.

artist - dancers, writers, designers, musicians and composers, athletes, film-makers.